THE
TEAM
SECRET

10 July 2023

Krysta,

To friendship!

Anton Butler

Koos Steadler.

THE
TEAM
SECRET

Accelerate your business with

SPECIAL FORCES

PRINCIPLES

Koos Stadler & Anton Burger

DELTA BOOKS

JOHANNESBURG & CAPE TOWN

All rights reserved.
No part of this publication may be reproduced or transmitted,
in any form or by any means, without the prior written
permission of the publisher or copyright holder.

Copyright © Anton Burger and Koos Stadler 2018
© Published edition Jonathan Ball Publishers 2018
Lightbulb graphic courtesy of Vecteezy.com

Originally published in South Africa in 2018 by
DELTA BOOKS
A division of Jonathan Ball Publishers
A division of Media24 (Pty) Ltd
PO Box 33977
Jeppestown
2043

ISBN 9781868428748
eBook ISBN 9781868428755

*Every effort has been made to trace the copyright holders and to
obtain their permission for the use of copyright material. The
publishers apologise for any errors or omissions and would be
grateful to be notified of any corrections that should be
incorporated in future editions of this book.*

Twitter: https://twitter.com/DeltaBooksSA
Facebook: https://www.facebook.com/DeltaBooksSA/
Blog: http://jonathanball.bookslive.co.za/

Cover by publicide
Design and typesetting by Martine Barker
Editing by Ingrid Delle Jacobson
Proofreading by Kelly Norwood-Young
Set in Stencil/Chaparral/Avenir/Caslon

solutions
Printed by **novus print**, a Novus Holdings company

*To Tyron Mansfield, one of the best team members
I worked with. I hope, no I know, you will recover from
your accident, pick this book up and be able to
read it without assistance.*

— **Anton Burger**

*To André Diedericks, Small Team operator
par excellence, who inspired me to go beyond.*

— **Koos Stadler**

CONTENTS

INTRODUCTION

This book is the brainchild of management consultant Anton Burger, who has planned and executed numerous projects in the mining, financial services, government and manufacturing sectors over a 19-year consulting career. Having seen all kinds of teams in action, Anton has first-hand experience of the principles and characteristics that make a team successful, as well as those that will likely cause it to fail.

During his career Anton often asked himself the question, why are some projects more successful than others? The answer came during a December holiday while lying in his hammock reading the book *Recce: Small team missions behind enemy lines* written by former Special Forces operator Koos Stadler.

Anton always suspected that he and his teams had unwittingly applied different – and often unconventional – techniques on some of the projects they had undertaken. But until that moment he had never defined the principles required for a team to be successful.

However, as he read the book he recognised a number of concepts that seemed familiar. Anton realised that the characteristics of the Special Forces small team as described in Koos' book, were the very ones that ensured several of the teams he had been involved with over the years were efficient and achieved their goals.

He was so excited, he ran into his house and exclaimed to his wife, 'I know now why we were successful in some projects – we used the same principles as the Recces!'

He then started to write down a few of the insights he had gained around successful teams. A few months later Anton shared his ideas with a friend, a published author, who immediately suggested that he write a book, to which Anton replied, 'Me, write a book? Never! I'm not a writer but I might consider it if I could co-write it with the author of *Recce*, since I lack the necessary military knowledge.'

To Anton's surprise the friend responded by saying he could easily arrange this. Shortly thereafter Anton met with his friend's contact, the indomitable Annie Olivier at Jonathan Ball Publishers, who promised to pitch the concept to Koos.

Curiously and purely coincidentally, Koos – who at the time was working halfway across the globe in a corporate business environment – had for some time been contemplating the idea of translating small team principles into business practice. Miles apart, Anton had been asking the same questions: What are the characteristics that made Special Forces teams so successful? Which principles were the guiding factors in these teams? What is the ideal team size? What are the required traits of a team leader?

And ultimately, could the principles of Special Forces small team operations be used in the private sector? Could they be applied to teams in the business and corporate environments? Because Anton had actually experienced business turnarounds as a direct result of these principles, he had no doubt as to their value in the private sector.

The character Jo-Jo Brown was born during the initial interaction between the authors, as well as the idea to illustrate the principles and characteristics of Special Forces operations and operators by telling the story of a Special Forces mission at the beginning of each chapter. Jo-Jo is the leader of a team that conducts Special Forces small team missions deep behind enemy lines. The larger-than-life José da Silva joins him as the team's second-in-command alongside team members Themo Rodrigues and Steve Seloane.

These characters are based on real members of the South African Special Forces who participated in missions hundreds of kilometres into enemy territory with Koos Stadler during the Border War.

In the book, once the team is deployed they face the typical challenges that a Special Forces team would encounter on a mission. As the story develops, the unique characteristics of Special Forces team members, as well as the principles of successful small team operations are unpacked, analysed and finally translated into business terms. The principles are explained further by means of case studies from the business world – actual experiences Anton has had in his consulting career. These case studies show the dos and don'ts for teams based on real-life situations.

In the final chapter, Koos and Anton also share their

thoughts around leadership, one from a distinguished Special Forces point of view and the other from that of a highly successful career in management consulting. Their conclusion is interesting but hardly surprising: successful teams are led by leaders who display specific character traits, use particular leadership concepts, take full ownership and lead through sheer conviction.

Around the world companies rely on different kinds of teams to grow and to achieve success. Just think of how ubiquitous teams are in your company – a single employee can rarely work as an island. Some teams are more formalised than others but when you think about it, nearly all businesses are composed of formal or informal teams.

Even a small start-up usually consists of a core group of founding members. Knowing the principles and characteristics of a successful small team can therefore also be an essential factor in an entrepreneurial venture.

In this book we hope to show you the different keys to unlocking the team secret – those principles that will help to improve the performance of the myriad teams operating in your particular environment and in doing so, ultimately accelerate and grow your business.

LIST OF ACRONYMS

AK-47   a type of assault rifle

AKM: Avtomát Kalashnikova modernizirovanny (Russian) tr. Modernised Kalashnikov Automatic Weapon (a modernised version of the 1940s assault weapon designed by Mikhail Kalachnikov)

ANC: African National Congress

CO: candidate officer

DET: data entry terminal

DR: dead reckoning

DRC: Democratic Republic of Congo

DZ: drop zone

E&E: escape and evasion

EQ: emotional quotient

FAC: forward air control

GL: general ledger

HF: high frequency

HQ: headquarters

Int: intelligence

IO: intelligence officer

JARIC: Joint Aerial Reconnaissance and Interpretation Centre

JLs: Junior Leaders

LEDs: light-emitting diodes

LZ: landing zone

MECSUP:	mechanical, electrical and chemical engineering support
OC:	officer commanding
OP:	observation post
Ops:	operations
PT:	physical training
RV:	rendezvous
SAAF:	South African Air Force
SAMHS:	South African Military Health Service
SOPs:	standard operating procedures
SSO:	senior staff officer
SWAPO:	South West African People's Organisation
SWOT:	strengths, weaknesses, opportunities and threats
UHF:	ultra high frequency
VHF:	very high frequency

1

THE SMALL TEAM CONCEPT

Captain Jo-Jo Brown lifts his head slowly from the backpack on which his chin has been resting. He is careful not to attract undue attention through sudden movement or by disturbing the wildlife around him.

He then tunes his ears to the sounds of the bush but cannot detect any noise aside from the shrill, monotonous screeching of cicadas. With measured, deliberate movements he scans the bush in his area of responsibility, the zone he has allocated himself after he placed his three other team members in an all-round defence when they established their hide at daybreak.

Jo-Jo observes the thick brush directly in front of him. In a practised manner his eyes move from left to right, covering all possible entry routes and hiding spots. He then scans the middle distance, searching the bush in a similar way from left to right as far as the vegetation allows sight. All seems quiet and undisturbed.

He glances at his watch, noting that it is 09:23, exactly 15 minutes before their scheduled radio call with the tactical headquarters. Jo-Jo turns his head to the left where he knows José da Silva should be. Their eyes lock. His team buddy is ready and waiting for his signal to prepare the radio. The antenna had already been positioned earlier that morning.

Da Silva winks nearly unnoticeably before Jo-Jo moves

crouched over towards the dark shadows of a tree with low-hanging branches outside their circle of defence – a position previously agreed on. From there he will listen out while Da Silva establishes comms (communications).

Once in position, he gives a thumbs-up with his left hand, his right hand maintaining a firm grip on the AK-47 while his finger rests lightly on the trigger guard.

Jo-Jo had prepared a message an hour before on the data entry terminal (DET), the electronic device that would be connected to the radio to transmit a coded message with their current position and future intentions to tactical headquarters. The high-pitched electronic clatter of the burst-transmission barely reaches his ears but he knows a trained ear would pick up the unnatural sound right away.

Four minutes later the scheduled radio call is over, the radio has been stacked away in its runaway bag and the antenna detached, ready to be re-connected in case of an emergency.

On Da Silva's signal, Jo-Jo slowly gets up and, checking that the bush in front is still quiet, makes his way back to his position. Halfway back he freezes.

Themo Rodrigues, the third member of their four-man team, has clicked his tongue. It was hardly audible but it made him stop dead in his tracks. Crouching low, Jo-Jo slowly turns his head in the direction of the operator lying with his back towards him, facing outwards. Themo twists his head towards him and shapes a word with his mouth.

But Jo-Jo already knows what he is trying to convey. Themo's left fist is up with a turned-down thumb … enemy approaching, close by.

♦

This story – based on true events – portrays something of what it takes to operate as a successful Special Forces Small Team.

The world over, Special Forces operations are conducted by carefully selected teams. As a rule, these teams are comparatively small – much smaller than the standard combat unit in a conventional military formation. Where the smallest sub-unit in a regular infantry battalion would be a section of ten, they would still form part of a platoon consisting of about 36 soldiers – a small headquarters element and three sections of ten each.

In most modern armies three platoons form a company, again with an HQ element as well as a support weapons element. Three companies combined, along with their HQ and fire support platoon, would constitute a battalion. In conventional warfare terms, a battalion comprises a unit; anything smaller than that is considered a sub-unit or a sub-sub-unit. Conventional wisdom prescribes that sub-units must function within the support blanket of the battalion, in other words, within reach of its indirect support weapons and in most cases within range of the formation's tactical radio (VHF or UHF) network.

Naturally, in a conventional military campaign, the unit deploys within the geographical space the formation is responsible for, either to defend or to launch offensive action. This restriction is paramount if the defensive line or the attack formation is to be kept intact and so as to ensure that the enemy does not force a breach in the defensive positions or succeed in enveloping or encircling the formation.

Special Forces teams, both in the South African context and across the globe, operate on different terms. Firstly, the battle space differs vastly because the majority of Special Forces missions are conducted behind enemy lines and not within the conventional sphere of operations. Secondly, the nature of the task is completely different since the team is expected to conduct a definitive task – a raid, a reconnaissance or a sabotage mission.

Thirdly, team members are selected and specially trained for their task and have at their disposal all the means (in terms of logistics, support and transport) to execute their mission. Last but not least, the team is tailor-made for the job, which invariably implies a small but highly effective group.

While the idea of small, highly effective teams is not unique to the South African Special Forces, the mould in which the two-man team concept was set locally differed somewhat from the more conventional approach. In the late 1970s operators from what was then 1 Reconnaissance Commando such as the larger-than-life Koos Moorcroft and legendary late André 'Diedies' Diedericks, introduced two-man teams for tasks previously performed by bigger teams. (Later, specialist reconnaissance sub-units known as 'Small Teams' were to form part of all the reconnaissance regiments with the exclusive purpose of conducting specialised missions using the two-man concept.)

For reconnaissance and certain types of sabotage missions, the two-man team proved to be a highly successful vehicle. These teams deployed for extensive periods – sometimes in excess of two months – hundreds of kilometres behind enemy lines, operating independently and clandestinely. The aim was to collect information or to destroy critical enemy infrastructure.

The reasoning behind this was that smaller teams could be inserted and extracted more easily and would be able to approach the target undetected since they would move quietly through the bush, hide away easily and leave fewer tracks.

The lessons in this book are not exclusively derived from the two-man team concept but from the notion that smaller teams are highly effective for certain types of missions. In the Special Forces context smaller teams – as opposed to large groups – have proved to be more effective in missions of a specialised nature.

We believe the same principle applies in the business world. Companies tend to use fairly big teams for anything from client services and projects to sales and business development. We will show that the principles on which a Special Forces Small Team operate and which make them such a success can be applied to teams working in small and major companies. The success of Special Forces missions can of course also be attributed to aspects such as greater motivation (due to the stringent selection process), specialised training and the use of superior arms and equipment. The strengths inherent to the team due to its comparatively small size should also never be underestimated. These inherent strengths include:

☐ Small team members are more alert. There is comfort in numbers, so the moment the assurance of human support around the individual is removed, he 'switches on' by default and accepts responsibility for his own safety.

☐ Small team members take ownership of their mission objective. Since there are fewer individuals to blame should the mission not be completed successfully, they have a tendency to take ownership of the success of the mission.

☐ Small teams move with more stealth and can hide easily. Owing to the two aspects described above, team members tend to take greater responsibility to anti-track (not leave a clear spoor), move silently, apply strict patrol tactics and enforce self-discipline within their hiding spot.

☐ Small teams move faster simply because it is easier to control a small number of people.

☐ Small teams adapt more easily to new challenges and have greater flexibility when adjusting to unexpected obstacles.

Special Forces' modus operandi, its strategic approach and tactical application are contained in a comparatively small number of confidential publications such as the *Minor Tactics Manual*, the *Small Team Reconnaissance Handbook* and a higher-order directive simply called *Special Forces Doctrine*. As the commanding officer of the Special Forces School (2002 to 2005) and subsequently as senior staff officer responsible for training at the Special Forces Headquarters, co-author and former Special Forces operator Koos Stadler was closely involved in rewriting and publishing both the *Minor Tactics Manual* and the *Small Team Reconnaissance Handbook* in 2005 and 2006.

The characteristics of Special Forces personnel, the very requirements that make them 'special', are summarised in the tactical manuals while the principles of Special Forces operations are analysed in the Special Forces Doctrine. During that time, the principles of Special Forces operations were deliberated and finally published under Koos's leadership, with international publications such as William H McRaven's *The theory of special operations* as guideline.

In this book Koos also presents his personal views on the characteristics of the people he closely interacted with during his Special Forces career. In addition, he discusses from a personal perspective the principles of Special Forces operations – those undeniable truths that are key to achieving success in any mission. Finally, he shares his views on leadership in Special Forces – those attributes that have made the difference in daring and highly sensitive missions.

For the purpose of this book's discussion about the advantages of employing specially selected team members in small teams rather than bigger conventional groups, the eight principles of small team operations as described in the Reconnaissance manual and derived from the principles of Special Forces operations, as well as the characteristics of Special Forces personnel, are summarised below.

These principles and characteristics will be discussed in greater detail in upcoming chapters and we will show how they can be applied to team members in a work environment.

Eight principles of Small Team operations:
- ☐ Outstanding leadership – transformational leaders who care and inspire
- ☐ Cooperation – working closely together as a team
- ☐ Mutual support – assisting and stepping in when a buddy needs it
- ☐ Knowing each other's strengths and weaknesses
- ☐ Planning together – essential to foster a sense of ownership
- ☐ Maintenance of the aim – no operation can have two aims – stick to the script!
- ☐ Commitment – a firm belief in the cause
- ☐ Rehearsals – each operation to be rehearsed down to the most minute details

Nine characteristics of a Special Forces operator:
- ☐ Dedication – a high level of dedication to task and team
- ☐ Ownership – takes full ownership of the job at hand
- ☐ Self-confidence – faith in one's own abilities

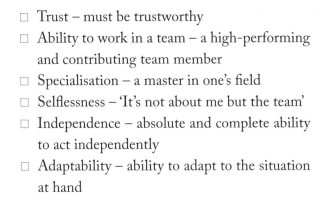

- ☐ Trust – must be trustworthy
- ☐ Ability to work in a team – a high-performing and contributing team member
- ☐ Specialisation – a master in one's field
- ☐ Selflessness – 'It's not about me but the team'
- ☐ Independence – absolute and complete ability to act independently
- ☐ Adaptability – ability to adapt to the situation at hand

A vast number of military principles can be applied to the way modern companies are run. For example, as every army needs a strategy for success and survival in battle, every organisation needs a strategy for success and survival in the business world. The strategy can be offensive – to gain market share, grow through acquisition or to launch new products. It can also be defensive – to protect market share or increase barriers to entry.

Companies need different battle plans to achieve their strategy and, like Special Forces teams, they need to function like a well-oiled machine firing on all cylinders.

However, modern companies have become so big and complex and the tasks so complicated that the execution of most tasks requires a group of individuals. A single person rarely possesses all the knowledge and skills required to perform certain tasks, hence the need for a group of people with the required knowledge and skills.

The team, instead of the individual, can be considered the DNA of many companies. Teams that make or do things, run things or recommend things play a pivotal role in achieving strategic and financial objectives.

Most organisations consist of formal teams that vary in size and perform tasks directed towards the attainment of organisational goals: teams such as advice and involvement teams (e.g. management teams, problem-solving teams, quality control circles); production and service teams (e.g. assembly teams, airline cabin teams, claims processing teams, sales teams, HR teams, mission directed work teams, self-directed teams, self-managing teams); project and development teams (e.g. software development teams, product development teams); virtual teams (e.g. teams that are located across cities or continents that use technology to communicate and do their work) and action and negotiation teams (e.g. military teams, emergency surgical teams, union teams).

The magic lies in developing and utilising these teams to their full potential so that they can make a difference and contribute meaningfully to an organisation. Key to this is that teams should be led by leaders who can inspire and motivate team members to climb that hill, plant a flag and claim victory.

We will focus on teams that are given tasks that must be completed within a specific time frame, for instance a set number of items by close of business or objectives to be reached by a specific date, and we will also investigate the difference in performance between larger and smaller teams. Our case studies are based on client interventions by a management consulting company that co-author Anton Burger worked for. During these client interventions he worked with and managed teams ranging from two to 110 people across various industries.

An interesting truth was revealed during two such client interventions several years apart when two teams, one large and one small, had to deliver the same type of solution. The smaller team delivered the work within a significantly shorter time frame and with a smaller budget. Over the 19-year period he worked with and managed teams the question was often asked, why are smaller teams able to achieve so much more? Let's look at the following example.

A big life insurance company wanted to computerise their business processes to improve operational efficiencies. This would not only bring down operational cost but also improve customer experience.

The management team of the organisation approached Victor Pereira (pseudonym), a management consultant, to assist with the selection of suitable software to computerise the business and to put a team together to implement the system. A system was soon selected and a seven-member team was established.

The team consisted of a team leader, a two-man development team, an IT expert and a three-man business analysis (to determine the needs of this particular business) and testing team. The members of the team were all specialists in their fields and had much experience.

Besides the normal challenges that go with a project of this nature, there was one additional challenge – the version of the software in question had never before been implemented anywhere in the world. The client would be the first!

Adding to this challenge was the fact that, should any software code issues come up, they could only be resolved by the software provider who was based in the United States. This meant the team needed to be flexible and had to work after hours in South Africa to coincide with the working hours of the software provider.

However, the project team took ownership of the challenges and was determined to solve the issues and implement the system. The relatively small size of the team made communication and decision-making easier. Each team member was adaptable, committed to the project goals, and took ownership. This ensured effective and high-quality deliverables. A combination of factors, such as the size of the team, the right people with the right skills and their commitment to the goals, ensured that the project was delivered four months ahead of schedule and R2 million under budget.

After the successful completion of the project, Victor was approached by the life insurance company to salvage a project to replace their outdated and disparate transactional systems (that had already been computerised) with a single modern system. The company had already spent some time and money trying to implement a new transactional system but little progress had been made. As project director, Victor was confronted with the challenge to restart the project and complete it within the original time frame with a smaller budget.

Given the time pressure, the company believed throwing a big team at the problem would help solve it. Up until this point in his career, Victor had predominantly worked with smaller teams and had never experienced the challenges surrounding teamwork in a team of this size.

A mixture of existing and new teams was assigned to the project. This overall team, totalling 110, was made up of multiple sub-teams ranging between four and 12, each with their own team leader. Multiple vendors supplied software components which had to be integrated with each other and existing interfaces.

The multiple teams and vendors, combined with a highly regulated financial services environment, created an extremely complex project.

The size of the greater team posed a significant challenge in terms of communication and coordination. Teams started planning their respective deliverables, sometimes without consulting or planning together with other teams that were involved. Some team leaders excluded team members from the planning process which meant that team members could not commit to time frames. This led to a lack of commitment with team members not taking ownership.

Consequently, the project struggled to gain momentum.

A project of this scale requires careful planning and coordination between different teams involved. Teams depended on deliverables from other teams to meet deadlines. For example, the development team could not start development unless the business analysis team had completed their business needs specifications.

The problems were exacerbated by the fact that team leaders did not have the right authority levels to make decisions on the spot and this also hampered progress.

One of the key teams started missing critical deliverables, which had a negative impact on all the other teams.

The moment non-delivery becomes a reality, pressure mounts for all parties involved. At times like these the level of trust among team members is the glue that holds things together. However, in this case there was a breakdown in trust among some members of the overall leadership team.

At this point Victor realised that at the current rate of progress the team would not reach the project goals. An intervention was needed. He red-flagged it with the managing director of the company and it was decided that a different approach in terms of coordination was urgently needed.

The project was stopped and the approach re-evaluated. The entire project was re-planned but this time with all the team leaders and team members involved. Victor was astounded by the complete about-turn in the team morale. This resulted in more realistic timelines and commitment from all team members which fostered a sense of ownership.

The project made good progress but sadly, due to the significant delays, the original launch dates could not be achieved and the project was over budget. Surprisingly (or not), the small team that was incorporated into the bigger team made excellent progress and delivered on their scope of work, on time!

The value of teamwork, the importance of managing teams well and even the effectiveness of smaller teams have been well documented and developed over the past 70 years. In the 1950s a more scientific approach was introduced to the concept of teamwork when two American engineers, Joseph M. Juran and W. Edwards Deming, took their philosophy on quality to Japan. They were invited by the Japanese Union of Scientists and Engineers to do something about the perceived poor quality of Japanese products.

Their thinking gave birth to the concept of Quality Circles – a system in which small teams of employees voluntarily come together to define and solve a quality or performance-related problem. Secondly, it led to Total Quality Management – a system of managerial, statistical and technological concepts and techniques aimed at achieving quality objectives throughout an organisation. This system expanded into teams with the relevant authority (at low levels) to make decisions.

During the late 1980s and early 1990s organisations across the globe were dominated by self-managing teams – relatively small and highly autonomous work teams that take responsibility for a product, project or service – and self-directed teams – small groups of employees who have day-to-day responsibility for managing themselves and their work.

Another type of team that is often used to improve organisational performance is a mission-directed work team. The aim of mission-directed work teams is to provide leaders and their teams with the skills to:

☐ Achieve high and continually improving levels of quality, speed and cost effectiveness;

☐ establish goal alignment and business focus;
☐ benchmark themselves against best leadership and workplace practices to identify and address high leverage areas for improvement in a systematic manner;
☐ create a visual workplace (the use of pictures, graphics and other images to convey information and meaning quickly and simply) to simplify the management of objectives; and
☐ achieve teamwork, participation and continuous learning.

Work teams have gained worldwide acceptance in organisations. However, while teamwork is essential to organisational performance, effective teamwork is often elusive. A decline in effectiveness is often caused by teams that are too big, teams that do not have a clear purpose or a structured plan or are made up of the wrong members. Teams that are not trusted with great responsibility and are not allowed much freedom to make their own decisions may also fail. Conflict, mistrust and poor leadership are often the leading causes of poor performance by a team.

Professors Martin Hoegl (head of the Institute of Leadership and Organisation at Ludwig-Maximilians University in Munich), Hans Georg Gemuenden (of BI Norwegian Business School, Oslo) and K. Praveen Parboteeah (of University of Wisconsin–Whitewater) investigated the effects of team size on teamwork quality among 58 software development projects. They found that the top five teams in terms of teamwork quality ranged in size from three to six members and the bottom five from seven to nine members. More significantly, on average, teams of three members achieved 63% of the teamwork quality of the best team, which is in stark contrast to teams of nine members which only achieved 28%.

However, despite an abundance of research and evidence that smaller teams are more effective, organisations still seem to prefer large teams. This is possibly due to a false belief that objectives can be achieved with a certain degree of confidence with larger teams. For many companies there seems to be comfort in numbers.

Effective teamwork can only be achieved by attracting the right team with the right members. A poorly constructed strategy or project can still be successfully implemented by a good team but the wrong team is a recipe for disaster. John C. Maxwell, an American author of primarily leadership books, wrote, 'Teamwork makes dream work but a vision becomes a nightmare when the leader has a big dream and a bad team.'

With this book we aim to tap into the knowledge and experience of Special Forces small teams and learn how these can be applied in the business world. Our premise is that small teams are more effective than larger teams in the context of a specific job that needs to be done within a predetermined time frame.

We will show why the best vehicle is a smaller group of selected and highly motivated individuals who join together for a task. While the book seeks to analyse the unique or individual characteristics of Special Forces small team operators and the team principles they lived by, the unique make-up of the team leader will also be explored. What are the qualities that make the Special Forces team leader so efficient and how can these qualities be applied in the modern-day business environment to achieve success?

We believe organisations can learn from and implement principles from the Special Forces where exceptional results are achieved with small teams. If they apply these principles, companies will be in a position to select the right people for their teams; they will restrict the team members to those who are required for the job; they will inculcate a certain ethos centred around team principles; and they will appoint outstanding team leaders who will help teams achieve the required objectives in the most effective manner.

Join us on a Special Forces Small Team mission as we seek to show how you can accelerate your business with Special Forces principles.

2

SELECTION AND TRAINING

For Jo-Jo Brown, fulfilling his dream to become a Special Forces operator did not happen overnight; it was a long and tedious road with many twists and turns. The Special Forces selection and training courses are notoriously tough and the vast majority of candidates who start the course either withdraw or simply do not pass the rigorous tests. Candidates who are not exceptionally well prepared mentally and physically will not make the grade.

Long before he even thought of joining Special Forces, Jo-Jo's career took a path that would unwittingly prepare him for the challenges and hardships to come and lay the groundwork for his life as a professional soldier. First there was the Junior Leaders (JLs) Course at the Infantry School in Oudtshoorn which he completed with his best friend Piet Pelser. During the long and arduous JLs both of them were selected to become officers. For Jo-Jo, the year at Infantry School was the toughest experience of his life thus far, perhaps because it was such a drawn-out and persistently demanding programme.

The harsh discipline, the never-ending early-morning inspections, the continuous abuse by a core group of abrasive instructors – in addition to the realities of training in extreme conditions ranging from sub-zero temperatures in the Swartberg mountain range to the almost unbearable heat of Oudtshoorn in the midst of summer – brought a dimension to Jo-Jo's world that he had never experienced while growing up in the small town of Kuruman. He had to face new challenges and breach new obstacles.

But deep down he knew that he had been shaped and tempered for these new trials and that no amount of swearing or humiliation would bring him down. On the contrary, during the training he soon realised that, once the going got tough, a deep-rooted determination would spur him on and a kind of quiet satisfaction would embrace him; they could never break him!

Without realising it then, the characteristics of self-confidence and dedication that he quietly portrayed during these times of external pressure, would stand him in good stead as a Special Forces operator in times to come.

Then there was the parachute selection and training at 44 Parachute Brigade in Bloemfontein, again with his friend Piet. In a sense, parachute selection was a breeze compared to the continuous hardships of the JLs Course. Jo-Jo and Piet trained together and were well prepared by the time they reported for parachute selection. They had been briefed extensively and knew exactly what to expect.

They arrived at 44 Parachute Brigade in Bloemfontein on a Friday afternoon, the weekend before the selection course would commence. Once they had been issued with their equipment and settled down in the barracks where they would stay with the rest of the students, they prepared their kit and caught up on some well-needed rest.

On the Saturday morning they made a point of doing the parachute battery tests on their own – in the same conditions as they would during the selection course. That morning they passed the tests within a comfortable margin but since they knew the selection could be severe and would bring its own share of surprises, they took care not to become complacent.

The selection course, which was every bit as intense and demanding as they expected, required all their focus and energy but both Jo-Jo and Piet successfully completed selection and could commence with the basic parachute training course, commonly referred to as 'hanger phase'. While the instructors had no mercy and applied a severe disciplinary regime, they were highly professional and dedicated to their job.

In the end the training was fun, especially once they had done their first jump and the initial fear was tempered. It was a new experience and that first jump gave Jo-Jo the feeling that a new facet of his progress had been conquered.

Having completed parachute selection and training they were granted a much-needed two-week break. Back at Parachute Brigade, candidate officers (COs) Jo-Jo Brown and Piet Pelser were appointed as platoon commanders but first they had to do an induction and an airborne operations 'Battle Handling' course with a group of 12 other lieutenants, COs and corporals who had passed the basic parachute course earlier on.

They were an enthusiastic and highly spirited bunch, always drawing attention by singing and shouting slogans wherever they went. Soon they were referred to as the Dirty Dozen, even by the troops in the companies that they were about to lead. At the end of the third week of the course, the Dirty Dozen were taken to De Brug, a training area outside Bloemfontein, for tactical manoeuvres. The first major exercise involved a night parachute jump and infiltration towards a target – an 'insurgent base' they would attack at first light.

Jo-Jo was appointed as team leader for the exercise. He prepared well and gave his orders from a sand model, taking care to task each of the appointed sub-unit commanders in detail. That night, after they had landed and regrouped, Jo-Jo experienced his first real leadership challenge.

One of the corporals, Simon 'Sixpack' Stevens, a stocky and rather self-confident individual who was appointed as a subordinate commander for one of the cut-off groups during the attack, did not agree with Jo-Jo's decision to start the march to their target immediately. He also did not accept the compass bearing Jo-Jo had instructed them to use and claimed to know the terrain, announcing that his cut-off group would take a shortcut to their location.

Stevens made his own appreciation of time and distance and convinced the five men who would form part of the cut-off group to follow his plan. They would remain in position and wait until the early morning hours when they would take his shortcut to their positions.

No amount of arguing or threatening could change Sixpack's mind as he insisted that his men were tired and needed to rest. He was a few years older than Jo-Jo and was clearly trying to prove his seniority. It came to a showdown – Jo-Jo reminded Sixpack and the rest of the dissident group that he was the appointed commander for the exercise and that they had to follow his orders, to which Six-pack responded that they would not follow flawed leadership since the CO was making the wrong decisions.

It was a stalemate but there was no time to be wasted and the attack force soon moved out towards the target. Sixpack remained in position with his five followers.

After marching for most of the night, the attack force reached the forming-up point well before first light. The instructors were there to receive them and take control of the attack, since it would be with live ammunition. Although tired, Jo-Jo was relieved that his navigation was spot-on and that they were in time for the next phase of the exercise. However, it soon transpired that the cut-off group was not in position and not responding to calls on the radio.

'Where's your cut-off group CO? Have you lost control?' the captain in charge of the exercise quipped.

Covering for Sixpack, Jo-Jo's response was that they had lost them during the long march and that he was sure they would soon be approaching their position. For safety reasons the attack had to be postponed since the location of the group was unknown.

It was well into mid-morning when they finally heard a faint call on the radio. One of the cut-off group was injured and had to be evacuated but it turned out that they were way off course, not anywhere near their planned positions and, in fact, right in the danger zone of the axis of attack.

Jo-Jo never reported the incident, neither did Sixpack bother to apologise. During the exercise debrief he maintained that they were delayed by the injured man and took the wrong route when they tried to reach help.

Soon after the exercise the young COs were promoted to lieutenant and appointed as platoon commanders. Jo-Jo now was master and commander of his own ship and felt like he was riding the high seas. Fortunately, Jo-Jo and Sixpack ended up in different companies, Jo-Jo as platoon commander in Alpha Company and Sixpack as platoon sergeant in Charley Company. They still saw each other regularly however and the clash during the exercise would not be the last in their turbulent relationship.

Jo-Jo settled in with Alpha Company and established himself as one of the Parachute Brigade's most promising young officers over the next three years. During that time his company was regularly called up for three-month 'bush trips' to the operational area in northern South West Africa (today Namibia), commonly referred to as The Border.

The parabat company on Border duty would be stationed at Air Force Base Ondangwa from where they could react at short notice to emergency call-outs. Two sections of eight paratroopers each, better known as Falcon sticks, were always on immediate standby.

While staying at Ondangwa during his third year as platoon commander, Jo-Jo had the opportunity to work with elements of 5 Special Forces Regiment, better known as 5 Recce – or more affectionately, the Big Five. The Recces would be deployed in small reconnaissance teams to locate enemy positions. Once the Recce team had the enemy in sight, or were fresh on the tracks of an infiltration group, the parabat reaction force would be called in for an attack or follow-up.

During those few months, Jo-Jo often had the opportunity to sit with the 5 Recce operators in planning sessions or occasionally meet up with a team in the bush. Every time he was impressed with the sheer professionalism and unbridled dedication of the men.

He had made friends with some of the 5 Recce leader group and often visited their camp at Fort Rev when he was not on immediate standby. His new friends, in particular an enigmatic young captain called Kokkie de Koning, had been urging him to do the Recce selection and join up.

It didn't dawn on him immediately as he had never considered himself a career soldier but, at the end of yet another trip to The Border, he was hooked. When he got back to Bloemfontein, he had made up his mind but Piet was still undecided. In the end, having listened to Jo-Jo's endless stories of their deployments with 5 Recce, Piet agreed that they should do the Special Forces selection together.

The Special Forces pre-selection programme consisted of a week-long series of tests done at the South African Military Health Services (SAMHS) Training College in Pretoria. About 300 hopefuls from all the arms of service across the country had gathered there. For Jo-Jo and Piet pre-selection was merely a formality as they had been preparing for two months and knew exactly what to expect.

To thin out the field, the physical tests were concluded first. These consisted of a fitness battery test (six different

PT (physical training) tests done in quick succession, not unlike the parachute battery tests), a 15 kilometre hike with kit and finally a range of biokinetic tests in the gym. These would be followed by a full medical examination and a series of psychological and aptitude tests.

Jo-Jo and Piet stayed together in a cramped little room at the end of a block of barracks at the SAMHS College. The pre-selection turned out to be not as demanding as they had envisaged and they both passed with relative ease.

As soon as they heard that they had passed the test series, they were instructed to report at 1 Recce in Durban. Of the initial 300 candidates only 30 were found suitable to continue with the Special Forces selection course. And so a whole new chapter in the life of the boy from Kuruman began.

By the end of May that year, the two friends drove to Durban in Jo-Jo's Toyota Corolla and into the gates of 1 Recce on the Bluff, with adrenaline pumping and mouths dry. Here they were at the centre of Special Forces training in South Africa, the very heart of the elite. They didn't know what to expect. They moved into the officers' mess where they soon met some of the mean-looking Special Forces officers who treated them – surprisingly – as equals, even though it was no secret that they would be doing selection.

Within a week the whole course moved to Dukuduku, a training area close to St Lucia, for Special Forces Orientation, a five-week preparatory course before the actual selection. The aim of this course was to level the playing field, since candidates came from all sorts of backgrounds, from different arms of service and some even from civilian life. The programme was primarily aimed at building up strength and fitness but it also addressed the elementary military skills of musketry, map reading and navigation, basic field craft, communications and weapon handling.

They marched further and with progressively heavier packs every week and the PT became more strenuous by the day. At the end of the programme 18 guys were left from the original group that joined for pre-selection. They were in top shape, physically fit and in good spirits. No selection could stop them now!

The Special Forces selection course was incredibly intense. The worst was the uncertainty, the fact that they never knew how long an exercise would last or when the suffering would end. Even so, the programme was too short for Jo-Jo to consider giving up. Over the course of the next three days they were exposed to a series of the most strenuous physical – and what was intended to be psychologically taxing – exercises.

A particularly challenging test was when a team of five had to carry a fuel drum filled with water over a distance of 12 kilometres. The team had to improvise a way to carry the drum with the aid of two logs and some rope. Since two of the guys in Jo-Jo's team were tall, they were carrying at one end while the 'shorties' (Jo-Jo and another shorty) carried at the other. The shorter guys ended up taking all the weight as the water in the drum tended to collect at the lower end of the contraption. This was sheer character-building stuff, as they were still carrying their full kit and rifles under the additional weight of the drum. The sand track was uneven under their tired feet and the end never seemed to come.

There were other exercises such as Octopus and Iron Cross which were physically demanding but since they were all group exercises, Jo-Jo found them relatively passable. The only really demanding test was the interrogation phase towards the end of the course. The instructors concocted a devious plan to capture them, one by one, as they patrolled through a stretch of thick undergrowth. With their arms tied behind their backs and their faces hooded, they were transported to the base where the 'interrogation' commenced – and lasted throughout the night.

During the course of the night Jo-Jo kept on listening out for a signal from Piet. He had last seen him on the back of the truck when they were captured but since the moment they were hooded and blindfolded, his senses were impeded and he could not identify any of his close buddies. Occasionally, when he thought that there was no instructor close by, he would give a groan or a shout in the hope that Piet would recognise his voice and get some inspiration from it.

After the interrogation, each candidate would again be blindfolded and taken back to his position. Soon, when day started to break in the east, they were rounded up and herded like sheep to a jail where they were locked up. They desperately tried to catch some sleep before the madness started again. Finally, once inside the jailhouse, the hoods were removed and a plastic bag containing their overalls was thrown into the cell. Piet was nowhere to be seen. From some of the other candidates, he gleaned that Piet had packed it in during the night; he couldn't handle the cold any longer and apparently asked to be withdrawn.

After the Special Forces Selection only 12 of the original 300 candidates were left. Jo-Jo had a strange sense of remorse when thinking of Piet. Somehow he felt that he should have been there for him, motivating and supporting him. But he also realised that it was every man for himself and that no amount of peer support would carry a person through once he has decided to withdraw.

As for himself, he never thought of giving up, only of how he would prove to the instructors that he was competent and that he would survive the next challenge. He had only one aim – to finish what he had started.

The Special Forces training cycle was designed to produce a highly skilled soldier who would be prepared for the demands of the specialised operations conducted across the borders of the country. It was a year filled with fantastic new experiences. The wealth of knowledge Jo-Jo gained on the different courses, the extraordinary people he met, the new technology they were exposed to, all added up to make it a year of high adventure.

Jo-Jo also met inspirational leaders of men, made lifelong friends and travelled most parts of the country. Over the course of that one year in his life he did the most intense training imaginable.

The next phase, after selection, was the Special Forces Individual course, once again in the Dukuduku State Forest. After Special Forces Individual followed Basic Parachuting, Small Boat Orientation, Guerrilla Tactics, then Medical Level 3, Air Operations and Basic Demolitions. At the end of the training cycle they would be flown to Fort Doppies in the then Caprivi Strip for Bushcraft, Tracking and Survival and finally Minor Tactics, first the eight-week bush phase and finally a three-week urban tactics phase.

Suddenly, now that they had passed selection, the candidates were considered part of the Special Forces family. Attitudes towards them changed overnight. There was to be no more shouting and swearing. Objectives were given in a calm and mature manner and it was up to the students to achieve them.

On the course they were introduced to Special Forces equipment – radios, backpacks, boots and an array of gadgets Jo-Jo was not familiar with. The content of the course focused on the application of weapons and equipment used by Special Forces. They were also exposed to a variety of foreign weapons and had the opportunity to apply them, firstly on the shooting range and later during actual exercises.

Fitness levels were maintained by two PT sessions per day. These were meant to build them up for the demands of the rest of the course and Jo-Jo found them quite enjoyable. While they didn't do any more route marches, the backpack was now a constant companion during exercises.

After Special Forces Individual the group returned to

1 Recce to prepare for the next three courses: Basic Parachuting at 1 Parachute Battalion in Bloemfontein, Small Boat Orientation at 4 Recce, Langebaan and finally Guerrilla Tactics at 5 Recce, Phalaborwa.

Since the 12 remaining candidates had passed the Recce selection, they did not have to do the Parachute selection again. Jo-Jo and five others were already parabat qualified and only had to do progressive jumps. At the time the Parachute Training Wing was short of instructors, so Jo-Jo was co-opted as instructor for the course and had a great time training his buddies in the hanger. Those few weeks in Bloemfontein, his old hunting grounds, were quite carefree and Jo-Jo used the time to maintain his fitness by taking long runs and doing hard physical exercise.

After the parachute course the group drove through the Karoo to 4 Special Forces Regiment in the Western Cape. The ocean was a new environment to most of them and would certainly bring new challenges. Jo-Jo secretly dreaded the thought of the icy waters of the Atlantic Ocean off the West Coast but the few weeks at 4 Recce turned out to be a great experience.

The unit was quite unique. Situated in the picturesque town of Langebaan, the main base with accommodation, headquarters, logistics and admin was the public face of the unit. Across the lagoon on the northern end of the peninsula was the secretive operational base at Donkergat, an area naturally out of bounds for the public, from where operations were launched and where all training was conducted.

In the days when whale hunting was still both legal and

lucrative, Donkergat used to be a whaling station and the operational base was built over the remnants of the old structures. In actual fact, the main quay was formed by concreting the hull of one of the old trawlers. It also had a quay specially designed for the docking of the South African Navy Strike Craft as well as the Daphne class submarines, both extensively used for deploying the Recces during operations.

For Jo-Jo, 4 Recce was a world apart. Not only was it set in an exotic environment, but it also had a different heart-throb. The sense of purpose and professionalism of both operational and non-operational personnel Jo-Jo encoun-tered there remained with him long after they had left.

The Small Boat course was no walk in the park, given the extreme cold water of the Benguella current off the coast and the fact that they spent the best part of their days and nights either in or on the water. In those three weeks they swam and kayaked more than any sound-minded person would do in a lifetime. They became quite adept at han-dling inflatables, the operational rubber boats and were exposed to various infiltration techniques from sea to land as well as through water courses like rivers and estuaries.

After completing the Small Boat course the group drove to Phalaborwa, a town bordering the Kruger National Park in the far northeast of the country, for the Guerrilla Tactics course. Here the students were exposed to doctrines, tactics and the history of various rebel movements in southern Africa. The idea was to recreate a guerrilla base to expose students to a setting that resem-bled a freedom fighter encampment. All activities were based on the routine in a guerrilla base.

Instructors from 5 Recce were the commanders and trainers and led the candidates in song, marching, weapon handling and tactics. The unit didn't have a shortage of soldiers that had been fighting for those very guerrilla forces that were once enemies, so the students got a good dose of indoctrination à la Karl Marx-style and had to learn slogans from old masters such as Karl Marx, Mao Tse Tung and Che Guevara.

Aside from learning about revolutionary forces' doctrine and tactics, the course provided an in-depth background on the origins and history of the freedom movements of southern Africa. A significant amount of time was also spent on politics in the unit's areas of operation during peace support operations, among others Burundi, the DRC (Democratic Republic of Congo) and Sudan, with specific focus on the Darfur crisis.

For the first aid course, Medical Level 3, the 12 students had to drive back all the way to Durban, since the programme was presented on the Bluff. Once again, the course was intense but at the same time of an exceptionally high standard. The course leader, a medical doctor, was a qualified Special Forces operator, while the two instructors were level 5 emergency responders. After the first week's theory lessons, the rest of the course was spent entirely on practical first aid work.

The first part of the next course, Air Operations, was also presented at 1 Recce. By now the bright lights of the coastal city didn't appeal to Jo-Jo any longer, as he had visited the operational units and was eager to finish the training.

The Air Operations course was a cleverly structured programme to expose students to all the intricacies of clandestine work with an array of fixed wing aircraft and helicopters. The course leader, a very experienced sky-diver and head of the air operations branch at 1 Recce, took them through the paces of working together with different kinds of aircraft.

The course covered a series of subjects related to cooperation with the Air Force. They learned to prepare landing zones (LZs) for various aircraft, choose and prepare a drop zone (DZ) for parabat drops behind enemy lines, call in aircraft for resupply or pick-up and control fighter aircraft during close air support in a combat situation.

Although Jo-Jo had worked closely and extensively with the Air Force while at Parachute Brigade, the exposure to the full range of SAAF (South African Air Force) aircraft was a new experience. He especially enjoyed working in con-junction with the fighter jets as it introduced a complete new dimension – and little did he know how handy it would come in during special operations later in his career. The programme was concluded with a practical phase, this time at the Hells Gate training area close to St Lucia, where the students put to practice all the procedures they had learned.

Basic Demolitions came up next. While the normal demolitions course presented by the School of Engineers was generally aimed at the destruction of large-scale infrastructure, the Special Forces course had a specific aim as it focused on sabotage – where a relatively small group of men would be required to infiltrate their target and render it unserviceable, causing maximum damage with the minimum amount of explosives. To achieve this, students were taught various techniques, ranging from the use of shaped charges to the correct placement of explosives. Another part of the training included improvisation techniques, where the operator needed to apply innovative ways of setting up charges with the minimum equipment at his disposal, or use improvised techniques to set time switches and booby traps.

A further addition to the course was exposure to custom-made demolition charges designed and manufactured by MECSUP, the highly specialised engineering company that provided mechanical, electrical and chemical engineering support to Special Forces units and worked exclusively on devices and equipment used in special operations. The MECSUP array of charges included various initiation devices ranging from time switches to light-sensitive and anti-tilt mechanisms. Students were also exposed to different forms of explosives, such as the very effective PE4, PE9 and Torpex used in Special Forces operations. The course was mentally demanding since they had to learn a number of mathematical formulae to work out the size and effect of charges. In addition, the pass rate for safety measures was 100% and no exceptions were entertained.

The day finally arrived when the group was deployed to Fort Doppies on the banks of the Kwando River in the Caprivi Strip for the final phase of their training. The nine months training cycle would be concluded with two courses – Survival and Minor Tactics. Six candidates from the previous selection course joined the 12 remaining students, bringing the total to 18.

To Jo-Jo's surprise, Sixpack Stevens, his arch-rival from the parachute induction programme, was one of the six. Jo-Jo was not even aware that Sixpack had passed selection and he had to contain himself so as not to show any animosity.

Ray Templeton, a seasoned operator from the erstwhile Rhodesian Selous Scouts, presented the survival course. On the very first day they arrived in the bush, their clothes and equipment were taken from them, leaving each of the students with only PT shorts, a T-shirt, a cap and a rifle to face the African bush and survive the chilly nights. Then they were taken by truck to a position about 15 kilometres from the survival camp and dropped off in the bush. Their shoes were also taken away and they had to cover the distance back to the camp barefoot. Jo-Jo couldn't comprehend the logic of this but realised later during the course that it was aimed at stripping them of all the comforts of civilised life and forcing them into survival mode from the outset.

Soon enough everyone started improvising by making rudimentary shoes from leaves, grass and strips of bark. Aside from providing protection against the burning hot sand, it taught them that makeshift feet covers could just as well serve as anti-tracking devices, since no clear footprint would be left. Wearing only PT clothes forced them to respect the bush, to move carefully around thorn shrubs and quietly through the undergrowth. For Jo-Jo, the result of those three weeks in PT kit under the African sun was that he would always take great care to move cautiously through the bush and to wear protective clothing during operations.

During the first week the student group established a base camp at the so-called Horse Shoe, a peculiar bend in the Kwando River, where they were given lectures on the wide variety of fauna and flora, their usefulness in a survival situation, what to avoid and what to exploit. Tracking formed an integral part of the course. After the initial lessons on spoor recognition, determining the age of a track, counting the number of tracks and eventually how to follow a spoor, they would always move out in two groups, the first laying a track and the second following. After a while it became second nature – to be aware of signs that would indicate human presence.

Over the heat of day and during the evenings the students received detailed lectures on the plant and animal life of the region. They learned how to identify edible plants as well as those to avoid. They soon got to know how to locate water in tree trunks or in the bend of dry riverbeds and how to produce water using a 'desert still', or a simple method called a 'tree still' utilising a plastic bag wrapped over the wet leaves of a branch.

Food was systematically reduced from one tin per day to nothing – as the students learned to set snares and traps for birds and small game. The Kwando River also provided a supply of freshwater mussels, while the small nuts from the dried-out fruit of the Marula tree provided some relief from the persistent hunger. Also in abundance during that time of year was the raisin bush, which provided edible berries as a meagre supplement to their almost non-existent diet.

At the end of the first week they were taken by vehicle

and dropped off individually in a remote area along the Botswana border. It was time for Exercise Egg – Ray Templeton's unique way of exposing the students to Mother Nature. Each was given two eggs, one match, a small piece of flint and two rounds of ammunition (meant only for protection against lions, which were abundant in the area). The idea was that they had to get a fire going, cook the eggs and sleep out alone under the stars.

Jo-Jo had spent countless nights in the veld on his own, so for him the experience was a positive one and merely a test of his ability to be completely at ease alone in nature. But for someone from the city who has not been exposed to the thrills of night life in the African bush, the experience could be quite frightening. After he had been dropped off, he went on a recce down a nearby omuramba (a natural water course or flood plain in the savannah terrain) and soon found water holes with some muddy water left from the rainy season.

He was hoping to make a crude wrapping with green leaves around his two eggs, then drench it with water, bury it under a few inches of sand and cook them by covering them with coals from the fire. But at the water hole he also found two rusted tins that he put to good use. He carried water in the tins to his 'camp', made a fire with a match and flint and simply boiled the eggs.

Before bedding down, Jo-Jo lit a second fire so that he could sleep between the two fires as a precaution against any hungry lion looking for a midnight snack. He piled up a sizeable supply of firewood, knowing that the coals would later die down. By the time the instructors arrived in the morning, he was refreshed from a reasonable rest and presented them with his boiled egg, having eaten the other the previous night. A number of the other students couldn't get a fire going and had a cold and scary night out in the bush, while most lost their eggs trying to cook them in the fire. One colleague discharged both his rounds at what he thought was a lion, then climbed a tree and spent the rest of his night trying to maintain his balance and get some sleep.

Back at base camp the students were soon in the routine of tracking, checking their snares in the evening and receiving lectures on a range of subjects. By now they were operating in full-out survival mode, receiving no nourishment for their emaciated bodies and still following a busy routine throughout the day.

Jo-Jo passed the theory and recognition exams easily, then went on to do the practical tracking evaluation. He found it hard to concentrate since he had started to experience fits of delusion as a result of malnourishment but in the end he managed to follow the track with relative ease and pass all the practical tests the instructors had concocted.

Minor Tactics, the final course of the year-long Special Forces training cycle, followed. In many respects the Minor Tactics course was more demanding than selection. When not patrolling with a 35-kilogram pack through the Caprivi bush, they were doing live-fire attacks, so the course became a long drawn-out battle with an 'enemy' who was persistently on their heels, with the 18 of them trekking and fighting consecutive battles day after day.

Slowly but surely they were shaped into highly effective

fighters. All the elements of bush warfare were incorpo-
rated – patrolling, stalking, observation posts, reconnais-
sance, ambushes, sabotage, raids, attacks, withdrawal
under fire, regrouping and counter attack.

To add to Jo-Jo's woes, he had to deal with his
relationship with Sixpack, who was as obstinate and defiant
as ever.

Somehow, during the escape and evasion exercise,
the final test of the bush phase, he ended up running
with Sixpack. The previous night the teams had to march
20 kilometres to reach the rendezvous (RV) where they
would be given new instructions. At 05:00 the next morn-
ing, having just reached the RV and not having slept at all,
they were called together and given their next RV – the
base at Fort Doppies, 40 kilometres further east on the
banks of the Kwando River.

They had the whole day, until midnight, to evade the
follow-up forces. They were told any student who got
caught would be summarily taken off the course. The
follow-up force was a company from 201 Battalion, the
Bushmen stationed in the Western Caprivi, supported by
2 Alouette helicopters and an array of vehicles and motor-
cycles. They were instructed to dump their rucksacks and
fill their water bottles. The company of trackers were
already in position and by six o'clock they could hear the
helicopters arriving from Mpacha. They were given one
hour to make good their escape and then the hounds
would be released.

Jo-Jo decided to gain a head start by going with the
rest of the group for the first 30 minutes, then he would

peel off, make a wide dog-leg to the south and anti-track to a position where he would wait until the main body of the trackers has passed. After about two kilometres he quietly slipped away from the rest, took off his boots and anti-tracked sideways only in his socks to a cluster of thick undergrowth. To his utmost surprise, Sixpack was also there, crouching low in the brush and grinning broadly.

'Lieutenant,' he said, 'so we meet again? We are destined to navigate together.'

Jo-Jo had no intention of joning up with anyone, so he started moving out to the south, taking care to anti-track every step of the way. But Sixpack had other ideas; he followed on Jo-Jo's heels, not bothering to take off his shoes or cover his tracks. When Jo-Jo confronted him, his response was that the trackers would not bother to follow a single spoor but would rather concentrate on the bigger group. It was a stand-off. By now the follow-up force was on its way and the choppers were in the air. There was no time to waste.

Suddenly an Alouette burst overhead, flying east in the direction the main group was heading. It did not circle back, so Jo-Jo knew they had not been spotted but he also knew that the trackers could not be more than one kilometre behind. From Sixpack's frantic efforts to stay with him, he could tell that the guy did not have the confidence to go it alone; he had to shake him off.

'You go in front, Sixpack. Lead the way south, I'll cover our tracks,' he said as he pointed south and started walking in that direction.

They could now hear the vehicles approaching from

the west and Sixpack did not need any further prompting; he started off at a trot. They kept going for about two kilometres, moving at a steady pace from thicket to thicket. While Jo-Jo could see that Sixpack made little effort to cover his tracks, he made sure that he left no clear footprint and disturbed as little of the bush as possible. When the time came, he did not want the trackers to know that they were two.

On the harder surface of an omuramba, they turned sharp left and headed east towards the river. They had barely moved a kilometre when they heard the distinct roaring of motorcycles from the point where they had entered the omuramba. Sixpack has increased his pace to just about an all-out run and Jo-Jo realised two things: firstly there was no way they could maintain that speed without exhausting themselves within the next few kilometres and secondly that they would leave a spoor like a highway while bulldozing through the bush – there was no way they could anti-track effectively.

When they hit another patch of dense undergrowth, he stopped in his tracks. Now was his chance. While listening to Sixpack tearing through the bush up front, he stepped sideways in his socks, taking great care not to leave a footprint or disturb the vegetation. This he maintained for a good hundred paces diagonally back from the direction they were running in. He knew he was cutting it fine, because by now he could hear the excited shouts of the trackers. The sound of the bikes was deafening and he could hear a helicopter approaching from the east.

Then he found what he was looking for – a cluster

of raisin bush with enough fresh vegetation to hide in. Ensuring he left no tracks, he stalked into the hide on his belly and carefully covered his body, firstly with dried sticks and leaves and then with fresh branches from the undergrowth.

They passed within ten paces of his hide, repeatedly. He could hear them calling commands and encourage-ment. Close to him someone shouted, 'Sergeant, there were two, I'm sure of it!' But then he heard them mov-ing off in the direction Sixpack had been running. About a kilometre further he could hear the Alouette circling and he knew his comrade was in trouble. He wasted no time to find out, as he knew that Sixpack would spill the beans and tell them about him.

Still taking his time not to leave any tracks he moved back west, in the direction from where they had come, knowing that the trackers would least expect him to return to the starting point. After a kilometre he began circling back south and kept a slow but steady pace to get out of the danger zone. As soon as he could hear no more sounds from the helicopters or motorcycles, he turned back on his original bearing towards the river.

He had enough water and maintained a leisurely pace for the rest of the day, even enjoying the scenery and the abundant wildlife at times. Twice he could hear helicopter movement north of him but they were too far off and he kept his pace. Just before ten that night he approached the base, exhausted but confident that he had passed. He took his time to move past the sentry points, as he did not want to get caught this late in the game.

By midnight all but four of the students had returned. It was soon rumoured that the four, of which Sixpack Stevens was one, had been caught.

The following day three of the missing students were back with them. Only Sixpack was taken off, allegedly not because he was caught but because he was singing like a canary after he had been captured; he had no qualms about spilling the beans on his fellow students.

Minor Tactics was concluded with a three-week urban warfare phase back in Durban. Now they concentrated on close-quarter fighting in built-up terrain, applying house-clearing techniques and hostage release actions. While heavy concentrated fire was required during contact in the bush, they now had to be cool, calm and collected, applying precision shooting combined with simultaneous and coordinated action.

Jo-Jo enjoyed the training but soon realised that he preferred the slow and calculated approach in the bush to the adrenaline-induced house clearing techniques. Besides, he had always felt more comfortable in the veld than in the city. Finally the day arrived for their passing-out, when the 17 of them would receive the operator's badge, the laureled dagger, during a small but prestigious parade at 1 Recce.

He had learned a valuable lesson from the encounter with Sixpack Stevens. Looking back, he realised that it had never been about running through the bush as fast as you could but rather the ability to master the pressure of the situation and apply appropriate measures to counter it.

While physical ability was always a top requirement, the mental agility to adapt to a situation was even more important. It now made sense to him why Ray Templeton, their survival instructor, would take away their shoes when the sand was too hot to walk on and why they sometimes had to lie for hours in ambush under the scorching sun; it was always about cultivating this mental ability.

◆

KEY LEARNING: SELECT SCIENTIFICALLY!

When a financial services company started a policy migration project they requested Victor's services. Policy migration from an old to a new system entails that existing policies with all the required policy information and historical transactions are transferred from one system to another. The transfer must be done in such a way that the impact on customers is minimised and the risk of financial loss is limited should customers leave the company.

The financial services company requested that Victor put together a small team of three and make them responsible for the policy migration project. Victor did not have much time to get the team operational so he called a few of his connections in the industry. He was soon referred to someone who came highly recommended for the job as team leader. During his interview this person came across as a strong candidate and his curriculum vitae showed the required experience.

Two team members with the necessary technical background were also recommended, interviewed and selected. The team started their work but it was soon evident that the team leader did not work well in a team and also lacked some expertise for the task at hand. Even though the other two team members were qualified and experienced, the team struggled to perform optimally. Victor had no option but to replace the team leader.

The change led to an improvement in the team's performance and they soon achieved a critical milestone. Further milestones were also achieved comfortably.

However, when the next phase of the project started there were a few delays resulting in a more stressful working environment. While the team performed well under normal conditions, one of the team members started making mistakes when the pressure increased which impacted negatively on the team. One night while burning the midnight oil at a critical point during a deliverable, this person just gave up and walked out on the team. This meant one person had to do the job of two and the team consequently failed to achieve the objective.

The team member was replaced with someone who had similar characteristics as the other two members. The team, now with only one original team member remaining, established the ground rules, got to know each other, settled down into cooperative relationships and started performing at acceptable levels in a very short time. The team was extremely resilient and managed the harshest work conditions calmly and collectively. They turned out to be one of the best small teams and achieved an objective that hadn't been achieved in ten years in the company!

In the Special Forces context taking a scientific approach to selecting operators was critical to the success of these elite units. The purpose of the selection and training course was to identify the very best – those individuals who portrayed the physical and mental stamina to cope with the demands of operations deep inside hostile territories.

The selection took place over a period of five days and thereafter the candidates who had passed were evaluated and tested over an 11-month training cycle under different conditions. This required quite an investment from the Special Forces and its instructors in terms of time but no effort was spared to ensure that exactly the right candidates passed muster.

The selection and training courses were adapted and refined within the first few years after the Reconnaissance Commandos were established. Initially there was a great focus on physical ability and endurance but it soon became clear that operators also needed the intellectual capacity and mental agility to cope with the pressures of the job.

Therefore, throughout the selection programme instructors and psychologists assessed candidates' individual qualities according to a comprehensive set of traits including their endurance under stress, ability to act independently as well as in a team, leadership and communication skills, initiative, spatial and sensory awareness and problem-solving abilities.

In the workplace, as in the military environment, tasks should be executed by teams that have been specifically chosen and are therefore right for the particular job. Teams that do not have the right combination of skills, knowledge and individual characteristics will not get the job done.

Nevertheless, companies often tend to select team members willy-nilly and then expect them to make important recommendations, manufacture items, perform specific tasks or manage complex situations. Why does this happen? Probably because the process to understand exactly what these required skills, knowledge and individual characteristics are is often time-consuming and costly. Many organisations are hesitant to put the required effort and resources into the selection process – to their own detriment.

Special Forces knew from the start that identifying the right individuals who could eventually become the members of an elite group of highly specialised soldiers takes time and effort. To create elite teams in your organisation similar input and dedication are required – there are no shortcuts.

So, how does one ensure that the right members are selected for a business team?

This can be achieved by putting a competency evaluation system in place. Typically, such a system is made up of four major components. Firstly each team member's role objectives must be identified, which in turn determine the competency profile required for that role. Once the competency profile has been established, the particular competency assessment tool/s or test can be selected. This enables companies to do an individual competency assessment and selection.

The role objectives are developed according to what an organisation wants to achieve and the tasks that must be executed by each team member. In the instance of a Special Forces team, the role objective of an operator is to conduct special operations against strategic targets in pursuit of national, political, military, economic and psychological objectives. These operations can be conducted during a state of war, a low-intensity conflict or in peacetime.

The required competency profile of employees can be likened to the nine characteristics of Special Forces operators. The selection of the competency assessment tool/s will be driven by the competency profile. In the Special Forces environment, examples of competency assessment tools include all the tests the candidates underwent during the selection course such as the psychological and aptitude tests, as well as exercises like Fuel Drum, Octopus and Iron Cross that test endurance.

There are a number of approaches and test batteries available to organisations to conduct tests and predict human potential in the workplace. The intention of this book is not to debate which one is best but to rather recommend that a company invest in one and put the required systems and resources in place to ensure that they can test and select team members on a scientific basis. For the purposes of this book, we'll use the SHL Universal Competency Framework™.

Competencies are defined as 'sets of behaviours (capabilities) that are instrumental in the delivery of desired results'. In the business environment, these competencies are the required actions and ways in which individuals complete specific tasks that support the attainment of organisational objectives'.

The SHL Universal Competency Framework™ has defined eight factors called the 'Great Eight Competencies'. These are eight competencies or abilities that can be used when testing employees to predict the likelihood of them succeeding in certain roles and environments. According to SHL, the eight competencies are as follows:

- ☐ The ability to systematically organise and execute plans, tasks, strategies
- ☐ The ability to take responsibility, give direction and to lead
- ☐ The ability to interact with other people inside and outside the organisation
- ☐ The ability to cooperate with and support other people
- ☐ The ability to apply own expertise to analyse and interpret information to resolve complex issues
- ☐ The ability to adapt to and cope with change or setbacks
- ☐ The ability to be enterprising and place value on personal performance
- ☐ The ability to be a creative thinker and be open to new ideas

A competency evaluation system can also be used to assess if already functioning teams have the right people. It will help the organisation to understand if a prospective or existing team member has the required competency levels to succeed in the role and achieve the organisation's objectives.

Such a competency system should be a collective effort between psychologists, line management and the organisation's human resources department. It must be noted that these tests only predict the likelihood of a person displaying the required behaviours. As already mentioned, it can be likened to the week-long Special Forces pre-selection programme where a battery of physical, medical, psychological and aptitude tests were conducted to thin out the field.

A person's true character will only become evident in a real working environment when he is confronted with a variety of pressures and challenges. For example, while Sixpack Stevens passed all the tests, his true colours only showed during the parachute induction phase and the escape and evasion exercise in the Caprivi.

Observing people before you select or employ them can be difficult but this challenge can be overcome. There's the option to hire the person on a contract basis or to include a probation period in the employment contract. This will allow employers to test and observe an individual under real working conditions.

As Jim Collins says in his book *Good to Great*, an organisation should hire people based on character rather than purely skills or education. With their motto of 'no dickheads allowed' the All Black rugby team also has a policy of selecting players based on individual characteristics.

They have been the most successful rugby team in history with an exceptional win rate.

In the following section we'll show how the Great Eight Competencies from the SHL Universal Competency Framework™ can be mapped to the Special Forces characteristics and how it can be used to assess and select team members in organisations.

NINE CHARACTERISTICS OF A SPECIAL FORCES OPERATOR	DESCRIPTION	GREAT EIGHT COMPETENCIES	DESCRIPTION
Dedication	A high level of dedication to task and team, more a personality trait than an acquired skill; strong elements of loyalty involved.	Organising and Executing	Plans ahead and works in a systematic and organised way. Follows directions and procedures. Focuses on customer satisfaction and delivers a quality service or product to the agreed standards.
Ownership	An attitude of, 'If I have to do this job, I take full ownership'; this is my responsibility and no one else's ...	Leading and Deciding	Takes control and exercises leadership. Initiates action, gives direction and takes responsibility.
Self confidence	Faith in one's own abilities – which only comes with knowledge and perpetual practice/rehearsal.	Interacting and Presenting	Communicates and networks effectively. Successfully persuades and influences others. Relates to others in a confident, relaxed manner.
Ability to work in a team	A high-performing and contributing team member who gets along with everyone in the team, respects others and is respected by others.	Supporting and Cooperating	Supports others and shows respect and positive regard for them in social situations. Puts people first, working effectively with individuals and teams, clients and staff. Behaves consistently with clear personal values that complement those of the organisation.

NINE CHARACTERISTICS OF A SPECIAL FORCES OPERATOR	DESCRIPTION	GREAT EIGHT COMPETENCIES	DESCRIPTION
Specialisation	Absolutely and undeniably a master in one's field..	Analysing and Interpreting	Shows evidence of clear analytical thinking. Gets to the heart of complex problems and issues. Applies own expertise effectively. Quickly takes on new technology. Communicates well in writing.
Independence	Absolute and complete ability to act independently as an individual, when the rest of the team is not present. This also goes with the responsibility trait – to carry the weight even if the team is not there.	Creating and Conceptualising	Works well in situations requiring openness to new ideas and experiences. Seeks out learning opportunities. Handles situations and problems with innovation and creativity. Thinks broadly and strategically. Supports and drives organisational change.
Adaptability	Ability to adapt to the situation at hand.	Adapting and Coping	Adapts and responds well to change. Manages pressure effectively and copes well with setbacks.
Trust	To be trustworthy … Exerting the assurance that others can rely on this person to get the job done; it certainly goes with the ability to trust others. While trustworthiness isn't one of the great eight competencies, it's an invaluable characteristic that is required of team members.		

(The Great Eight Competencies can be broken down into further detailed dimensions. For more information about this see the addendum at the end of the book.)

A short-term insurance company wanted to determine if the right people were leading their claims servicing teams. They approached Victor's company to assess the competency levels of ten team leaders, put in place a training programme to develop any competency gaps there might be and then re-assess the individuals after the programme to determine their progress. Victor suggested a four-phased approach.

Phase 1 focused on assessing these individuals' roles to select the relevant competency profiles. The output of this exercise was used to put together the applicable assessment tools to test their competency levels. Training material was developed and in addition, a benefits realisation model was designed to ensure progress could be tracked on operational performance and individual competency levels.

The team leaders engaged in various tests and exercises during Phase 2 to determine abilities and on-the-job performance. Reports were compiled and feedback was provided to the individuals and management team. One person was found not to be suitable for the role.

Overall operational performance was also measured and this, together with the competency level measurements, was used to populate the baseline measurements in the benefits realisation model.

Phase 3 was the most intensive phase. The individuals were put through a five-day training programme, followed by two months of intensive daily on-the-floor coaching and observations. During this phase they got the chance to put into practice all the theory they had learned in the training phase.

Some of the individuals got apprehensive as they were pushed outside of their comfort zones. Victor remembers one saying, 'I have been doing this job for ten years; there is nothing new you can teach me. Quite frankly, you are just wasting our time!'

Then there was a female team leader who hardly ever left work before 19h00. These two team leaders were also linked to the two teams that performed the worst.

Over time the coaches started building a closer relationship with the individual team leaders. More importantly, they went through a learn-by-doing cycle where they got the chance to implement their new-found knowledge in a real environment. They started to get feedback on the results of their actions and the opportunity to reflect on the whole experience. If the outcome or the experience was positive then the person was likely to change behaviour and adopt the new techniques as this worked better than the old way. To get to this point usually took a while. Most of the team leaders started adopting the techniques and it became second nature.

The observations continued during Phase 4. Certain techniques were reinforced and constant measurements were taken for the benefits realisation model.

Victor remembers the day the lady who could previously only leave work at 19:00 started to go home at 16:00. This was made possible due to the new operations management techniques the team started using from the training and specifically the daily stand-up meeting where team members started taking ownership of their work. While her husband was momentarily confused by the fact that she was home so early, her family was grateful for the extra hours they now had with her.

The 'ten-year know-it-all' individual also made an about-turn and confessed that this was the best learning experience he had ever had! The individuals were also re-assessed on their competencies 14 months after the original assessment.

The effectiveness of these leaders improved, therefore the effectiveness of the teams that they managed improved, resulting in an overall organisational performance improvement. Overall 19 (86%) of the 22 key performance indicators showed improvement. Twelve (55%) of the key performance indicators reached the target performance. All of the team leaders improved their individual competency scores and the improvement ranged between 1% and 53%. (The 53% improvement was the 'ten-year know-it-all' individual). There was also an improvement in the overall average of the group's competencies with a minimum improvement of 2% and a maximum of 20%.

 ## KEY LEARNING: LEARN BY DOING!

Special Forces training was designed to produce a skilled and prepared individual by providing him with all the relevant knowledge. The candidates had the opportunity to implement this knowledge and learn from the experience.

Jo-Jo gained a wealth of knowledge and experience on the different training courses. Daily lectures on survival, followed by practical implementation in the bush eventually led to a situation where the trainees could survive entirely from the bush as all their rations were taken away. The continuous live-fire attacks turned them into highly effective fighters.

Proper training can be powerful but it's a fact of life that many people struggle when they are asked to implement newly acquired knowledge or skills. A key reason for this limitation is that individuals are seldom taken through the complete learning cycle, in particular through a reflective learning opportunity. This severely limits people's ability to learn at a level that empowers them to handle complex challenges that are more abstract and less defined.

Training should therefore be based on experiential learning, as described in DA Kelb's book. This is 'the process whereby knowledge is created through the transformation of experience. Knowledge results from the combination of grasping and transforming experience.'

In organisations, a team member's learning is optimised when learn-by-doing is part of the learning process. The learn-by-doing cycle begins with an experience the learner has, followed by an opportunity to reflect on that experience and draw conclusions from what they have experienced and observed. The goal is for individuals to then test or experiment with different behaviours in the future. This begins the cycle anew as learners have new experiences based on their own experimentation.

True learning leads to relatively permanent changes in knowledge, skills or attitudes of individuals or teams.

Jo-Jo experienced his first leadership challenge when he was appointed as team leader during the parachute induction course. This experience enabled him to change his approach and identify solutions that would ensure a more favourable outcome in a similar situation.

In his book *The Seven Habits of Highly Effective People*, Stephen R. Covey writes about the principles of growth and change, 'In all of life, there are sequential stages of growth and development. Each step is important and each one takes time. No step can be skipped ... It is simply impossible to violate, ignore, or shortcut this development process. ... This is the single most powerful investment we can ever make in life – investment in ourselves, in the only instrument we have with which to deal with life and to contribute. We are the instruments of our own performance and to be effective, we need to recognise the importance of taking time regularly to sharpen the saw in all four ways.'

From Jo-Jo's selection and training and Victor's experiences in the business world, a few key points stand out:

☐ Invest in a system and process that allows for the scientific selection of team members – the investment will pay for itself!

☐ Adults learn best when they get to put theory

into practice and experience how doing things differently works better – practice makes perfect.

3

PLANNING AND PREPARATION

With practised ease Jo-Jo Brown goes down on his knees, skilfully blending in with the meagre shadow a young mopane tree provides. His ears are pitched, ready to pick up any sound. Earlier that morning he had deliberately selected the thicket with almost impenetrable undergrowth for their scheduled radio call. Now the thick vegetation limits his view. While it is a good hide, it does not provide sufficient view of their approach route.

His eyes scan the bush beyond the perimeter of their hide. Sweat has run down his forehead into his eyes, making it even more difficult to observe beyond the limits of their temporary base. Out of the corner of his eye he glimpses Themo's coiled figure, expertly camouflaged and completely hidden from any unsuspecting eyes. Jo-Jo knows exactly where his two other team members are even if he is not able to see them. In fact, in his mind's eye he can already visualise their posture, precise course of action and axis of attack should the bullets start flying.

For several minutes he remains on his knees in a crouched position, anxiously waiting for Themo to initiate fire or to signal a status update. Minutes feel like hours as his body starts aching from the severe tension and being in such an uncomfortable position.

Then suddenly Themo's white smile flashes relief as he

half-turns his head and forms the word 'gone' with his lips. His left fist goes up into a thumbs-up as he passes the signal on to the rest of the team.

When he finally relaxes, Jo-Jo realises how, during those tense moments of readiness, he has imagined a range of different scenarios and the course of action he would take for each. Even though they had prepared and rehearsed for just about any situation, the fear and tension remain.

Still crouching, he moves towards Themo's position and lies down beside him. 'What's up?' he whispers. 'Did you see them?'

'I think it's a hunter,' Themo says in a hushed tone. 'He had an old rifle and it looked like he was following game tracks.'

'Did he see us?'

'No,' Themo answers confidently. 'He passed over our tracks but did not seem to notice. And he went downhill towards the village.' Themo points in the direction of the valley from where they have been hearing sounds of the local population going about their daily business.

Jo-Jo lies back and considers their predicament. He does not want to take any chances so close to their target. While he knows they cannot risk moving in daylight, he also does not want to take any chances with the hunter or the inhabitants of the village.

Experience has taught him that very few things escape their vigil. Any disturbance or any change in their environment – especially a foreign track – is sure to be noticed. Since the locals invariably act as the eyes and ears of the militia, any sign of intrusion will be reported.

'Okay, we'll stay until last light but you keep a lookout,' Jo-Jo instructs Themo. 'No cooking, no movement. We can eat on the route tonight.'

After he has conveyed the message to the other two, José da Silva and Steve Seloane, he moves back to his position and settles down to wait for darkness. There his mind takes him back to their rehearsals during the preceding months – the contact drills, patrol formations, night work, stalking, long hours of practising emergency procedures and escape and evasion plans – night after night. During the day, there had been murderous PT sessions and lots of planning. Their mission is not an easy one ...

Their target is a strategic enemy air base 180 kilometres into enemy country. It is the main staging point for aerial attacks against own ground troops.

At any given time no less than 24 MiG-23 fighter aircraft are based at their target. As there are no fortified revetments (a barricade of earth or sandbags set up to provide protection from blast or to prevent aircraft from overrunning when landing), the aircraft are all parked on the apron at the two extremes of the 2.8 kilometre-long runway. Sixteen MI-24 attack helicopters, a few MI-8 support helicopters and an assortment of civilian aircraft line the taxiway adjacent to the terminal buildings.

Large amounts of cargo are also delivered on a daily basis by different types of transport aircraft. The enemy's logistics are mainly based on air transport due to the vast distances supply vehicles need to travel through guerrilla-infested jungle, where they also inevitably face the threat of landmines and ambushes. Thus, a variety of

Antonov transporters are parked on the apron.

Their task is straight-forward enough: do a final reconnaissance to re-affirm the location of aircraft positions and enemy concentrations. Then set up specially designed flares that would be command-detonated by bomber aircraft on final approach. Move out to the high ground overlooking the target on the southern side to monitor the attack and, once it gets light, report on the effect of the bombing.

The command-detonated flares have to be planted at three pre-determined positions west of the base, two at the northern and southern extremities of the western perimeter and a third exactly 1000 metres away on the aircraft's run-in. The challenge is to reach the target and complete the tasks in the allocated time given the extreme nature of the terrain, the weight of their packs and the severe restriction on water.

Two nights before they had parachuted in onto an unmanned DZ in a comparatively flat stretch of savannah – and had managed to regroup in the scanty moonlight with no injuries to the team. From the DZ they had had to cover 40 kilometres to their target on foot – moving only at night and hiding during the day. The terrain was uneven and unforgivingly hostile; densely vegetated valleys made way for steep rocky outcrops. This has made their progress during the darkest hours of night exceptionally slow.

On top of that, their packs are in excess of 60 kilograms. The heat and humidity down in the valleys have been sucking their bodies dry in a very literal sense. There is no water. At least, there is no water they can easily access, since the only potable water sources are used by the local population in the villages. Every step of the way they have had to apply stringent anti-tracking techniques – not a single footprint or any sign of their presence could be left.

For two months they had prepared for the mission. Intelligence sources indicated that an enemy build-up was steadily leading to an offensive against own forces. It was estimated that the offensive would be launched by mid-September, by which time enemy combat units would have reached peak form. The numbers of fighter aircraft and combat helicopters at their target would be at the maximum the air base could accommodate.

The planners had concluded that early September would be the critical time to launch a major bombing raid to destroy all aircraft on the ground. This operation would coincide with simultaneous actions by other specialised units to destroy two bridges and severely disrupt logistical supply efforts.

The job to lead a four-man team to the target and execute the mission had landed on Jo-Jo Brown's shoulders mainly for three reasons. Firstly, he has intimate knowledge of the terrain and the target area since he has operated extensively in that area before. Secondly, he has successfully completed the forward air control (FAC) course which has entitled him to direct fighter aircraft onto a target from a position on the ground. Thirdly, even though this information hasn't been overtly shared with him, the young captain is considered a rising star in the Specialist Reconnaissance Group, or Small Teams, of their unit. Frankly, there was no better choice.

The same could be said for the rest of the team

hiding in the thicket under the scorching sun. They are the cream of the crop. For Jo-Jo, it was easy to select his team members. Da Silva had been his team buddy for the previous two years. Together they had been deployed on numerous highly sensitive missions; he trusts the big man with his life.

Da Silva hails from mixed-race parents from central Angola. He is Portuguese speaking and has a personality as dominant and overbearing as his large frame. Besides his skills as an explosives expert, the man has a knack for radio work. He carries the huge Syncal 30 radio with the utmost ease – and can ensure a loud and clear signal under the most demanding conditions. Despite their differences in background and personalities, the two operators are inseparable.

Themo Rodrigues and Steve Seloane were buddies from another team. Steve's field of expertise is in medicine. He qualified as a Level 5 operational medical orderly and on more than one occasion has stopped short only of conducting open-heart surgery out in the field. He is a dedicated and loyal small team man with a sense of humour that can turn any tense situation into a chuckling contest. Since the start of the rehearsals Jo-Jo has realised exactly what an asset Steve is and has given him free reign to inspire the team through his optimistic outlook and witty remarks.

Themo is in a class of his own. As an operator, he is known as an all-rounder but his true skill lies in his abilities in the bush. A master-tracker, he can recognise the most inconspicuous sign and read it like a book. His ability to blend with the bush and become part of nature is almost superhuman. His anti-tracking skills have been honed to such a fine art that no other tracker will be able to find his spoor where he has passed through on patrol. An extraordinary sixth sense warns him of danger long before the others have noticed anything out of the ordinary.

The four operators form a formidable, closely knit team. The weeks of intense rehearsals have sharpened their senses and brought them to a point where they now know each other's strengths and weaknesses. Jo-Jo is content that they will now operate like a well-oiled machine. He would not have picked differently.

The same day he had received the operational warning order from the unit's commanding officer (CO) he'd had to make a call on the team's strength and composition – and convey it to the CO. The initial operational instruction mentioned a six-man team but given the nature of the task he'd had his reservations.

A team of six operators packs a solid punch and can certainly make a stand in a firefight but given the aim of the operation – a clandestine infiltration of the target where their presence won't be compromised – he had considered the team to be too large. If the mission was to be for reconnaissance only, a two-man team would have been ideal.

He had sat down with Da Silva that afternoon and, without sharing the details of the target, discussed their options. The broad scenarios were easy to convey as they had dealt with numerous similar situations before. While his buddy felt two men were sufficient to conduct a recce mission, they still had to consider the amount of equipment and the additional responsibility of planting the devices. In the end they had agreed that a four-man team would give them enough flexibility to do a clandestine infiltration, execute the reconnaissance and conduct the additional tasks.

The choice of individual team members was an easy one. Jo-Jo had just been about to start convincing Da Silva of what a great asset Themo would be during the reconnaissance phase when the big man had lifted both his hands and grinned broadly.

'Captain, don't even tell me! I know you want Themo ...'

Jo-Jo had been completely taken by surprise. 'Why, what's wrong with him?'

'No, no, nothing wrong with Themo, he's the right man,' Da Silva had responded quickly. 'I simply mean that I was expecting you to pick him. He's my first choice too, you know.'

It went without saying that Steve Seloane would join the team. Since he was Themo's team buddy and one of the best ops medics the unit has ever had, they hadn't needed to look any further. That afternoon he had checked in at the OC's office and conveyed the message – it would be a four-man team consisting of himself, Sergeant Da Silva and the two Corporals, Themo Rodrigues and Steve Seloane.

'You sure?' Colonel Tim Yalo had asked and that was that; no further argument and no challenging of the young Captain's wisdom on matters of operational pertinence. Such was the level of trust among the men of 5 Special Forces Regiment that the Colonel unconditionally accepted the Captain's choice.

Without delay he had picked up the secure phone on the small table beside his desk and pressed the only option, the one that would connect him to the General in command of the South African Special Forces. He immediately recognised the rasping voice, one not unlike an angle grinder at full blast, at the other end as the General demanded, 'Yes, Yalo, what's so urgent?'

'General, our choice is four. And the lucky draw for class captain is Jo-Jo Brown, as you suggested.'

The General had responded without a moment's hesitation, 'Why not six? Do they understand all the implications?'

While he was speaking to the General, Colonel Yalo's eyes had been fixed on Jo-Jo's. Then he had winked almost imperceptibly and said, 'You know General, you can't argue with these captains. The bugger has made up his mind.'

The deal was done. The rest of the conversation had covered admin arrangements, logistics, timings for operational and intelligence briefings and a date set for earliest time of movement. All gears would engage to initiate the planning phase. All systems would kick in to support the team in its preparations. The grind had begun.

Jo-Jo wasted no time discussing the operational framework with his close friend and mentor Major Danie 'Kokkie' de Koning, commander of the Small Team group, who would also be acting as operational commander for the deployment. As such Kokkie would be in charge of the tactical headquarters, deployed to the forward operational area. From the outset Kokkie had been briefed on the details of the mission but had the sense to leave the team's size and composition to the team leader.

He also wanted Jo-Jo to get the exposure of briefing the boss and making his own command decisions. Kokkie didn't challenge him on any of his decisions but prompted him in a subtle way to be critical and weigh up all his options. He expertly guided Jo-Jo in setting up a framework for his time-versus-task schedule.

Jo-Jo's first job that night was to do a detailed appreciation of the tasks to be conducted against the time available before deployment. There was much to do and from previous experience he knew that the solution lay in simultaneous action. While he attended intelligence briefings and liaised with the Air Force and other support services in Pretoria, Da Silva would initiate the team's logistical and communications preparation. Eventually it would be a fine balancing act, since he had to involve the whole team in the detailed planning of the execution, especially when it came to their actions on target and – in particular – the team's escape and evasion plan.

One of the critical aspects to keep in mind was that their rehearsals would require time together. While planning and preparation were necessary factors in the build-up towards deployment, rehearsing each contingency was the glue that pulled the team together into a tight and effective tool – and which would largely determine the success of the operation.

That night he had burned the midnight oil. He needed to present his time and task appreciation to the Ops (Operations) room first thing in the morning, since they had to coordinate all liaison visits with the Ops Officer at Special Forces Headquarters in Pretoria. Jo-Jo's list of entities to visit was endless and the sooner appointments could be tied up, the better.

His first stop in Pretoria would be the intelligence department at the HQ where he would receive initial briefings on the current war situation as well as an overview of target and terrain. The intelligence officer dedicated to the mission would also put him in touch with JARIC, the Joint Aerial Reconnaissance and Interpretation Centre, to study the latest aerial photos – or even submit a request for a new photo run. Liaison with the South African Air Force would be critical as he had to coordinate their requirements for the parachute infiltration, their escape and evasion plan as well as their extraction by helicopter.

He would also need to liaise with the medical liaison officer from the Military Health Services appointed to provide the medical support they required. Another critical support structure he had to get in touch with, was the specialised engineering group, MECSUP, which would provide technical training on the command detonated flares the team would be taking to the target.

A more pressing matter however, was to get the team together for their warning order. By the time he briefed them, the sequence of events had to be clearly planned and dates firmly plotted. From then on it would be Da Silva's responsibility to coordinate logistics and prepare the team's equipment. A critical part of his job was the planning and preparation of radio communications. For this he would work closely with Dave Turner, the Small Teams' signals expert.

They were fortunate to have Sergeant-Major David

Edward Turner, nicknamed 'Det' – his initials but also wordplay on the Data Entry Terminal used for burst transmissions. Dave was the Group's Warrant-Officer and also the communications expert responsible for setting up the tactical headquarters (tac HQ) for deployments. While he would guide Da Silva in preparation of the tactical radios to be taken along, the responsibility for drafting the operation's communications plan would rest with him. Det would also be responsible, in close cooperation with Kokkie, for preparing and packing the base-station equipment for the tac HQ.

Major Kokkie attended the warning order briefing, along with Sergeant Major Det and the unit's intelligence officer (IO), Major Thabo Thabang. Kokkie gave them the usual counter-intelligence brief about the need for secrecy and the accompanying death threat should anyone be found guilty of loose talk, after which Thabo provided an update on the war trends over the past week. The specifics of the target were not mentioned.

Then it was Jo-Jo's turn to sketch the broad nature of the task, now clearly defined as a reconnaissance mission, their method of infiltration and extraction, distances involved and time frames until deployment. Specific tasks were issued with regard to equipment acquisition and preparation, which included radios, medical packs, weapons and ammunition, personal equipment and reserve stocks to be prepared.

Then he specified the dates they would be getting together for rehearsals, tentative training dates with MECSUP as well as dates for final briefings and rehearsals in Pretoria.

There were no questions, as everyone knew that they would be working very closely together over the coming days. A sense of purpose gripped the team and everyone had silently formulated his own schedule.

For Jo-Jo, reflecting on the previous two months, the planning and preparation phase seems a blur of activities. He'd had two days to sort out his personal kit before he was off to Pretoria – along with Kokkie and Thabo the IO.

The latter had proved to be extremely efficient in networking and collecting information from somewhat unconventional sources – having been a guerrilla fighter during the struggle days himself. Intelligence briefings were thus supplemented with source reports from people who actually hailed from the target area, ranging from ex-prisoners of war to current members of the opposition partisan forces.

The close cooperation with JARIC turned out to be an eye opener as he had not expected the advanced technology levels – and indeed the competency of the photo interpreters – they were exposed to. There were satellite imagery and three-dimensional aerial colour photo-sets (aerial photos taken from different angles and superimposed to create a 3D effect) that in a very literal sense brought the surface of the earth to life. The target suddenly became a visual reality and he found himself immersed in 'flying' the optics over the terrain.

They spent a full day at MECSUP's facilities north of Pretoria. It turned out that the flares were huge cylinders with an explosive charge that would detonate the incendiary chemicals to produce a brilliant white light that could be recognised by an inbound aircraft from as far as 80 kilometres away. For the charge to be initiated each flare had a radio receiver connected by plug-in wires; once the pilot initiated the signal, the receiver would send an electrical pulse to the detonator and the flare would be ignited. Since it was a rather potent explosives device, safety procedures would form an essential part of their training.

During those five days in Pretoria, Jo-Jo checked in twice daily with both Det and Da Silva, not only to get an update on preparations but also to give them a status report of his progress in Pretoria. The truth was he was dying to get back to the team to get stuck into the real preparation – when they would spend hours and hours together to plan their route, rehearse their actions on target and practise their emergency drills. Day by day he made endless notes on items that he had to remember or techniques they had to incorporate in the rehearsals.

Back at the unit they wasted no time in getting their kit loaded for a two-week rehearsal stint at Leopard's Ranch, a secluded military area ideally suited for tactical manoeuvres away from the public eye – and indeed away from the unit where rumours could easily find a foothold. The cover story – a precaution to ensure that colleagues and family would not have any reason to start probing – was that they would be on a routine exercise to practise small team techniques.

An intensive regime of rehearsals followed, with the team practising and honing their tactical skills night *after night. Jo-Jo started off with patrolling skills, including stealthy movement, anti-tracking and camouflage and concealment but soon moved on to stalking techniques and penetration of a target. Much time was spent on testing contingencies and emergency drills within the team. Everyone was involved in drafting the emergency plan and E&E (escape and evasion) procedures.*

Throughout the rehearsals, radio procedures were meticulously tested; every team member had to establish communications under various demanding conditions. Similarly, under the watchful eye of Steve Seloane, their medical skills were fine-tuned. Quite regularly, a buddy was 'wounded' and had to be carried out of a firefight and treated in the heat of battle.

During week two of their rehearsal Kokkie, Det and Thabo joined them. Details of the target were finally shared with the rest of the team during an updated intelligence (Int) briefing. Now planning of the execution phase could start in earnest. Thabo had brought maps as well as stereo photo-sets (pairs of pictures that, when viewed through a stereoscope, create a three-dimensional image) of the target area and wasted no time to set up an Int/ Ops room in one of the bunkers. Bent over the maps and photo-sets during the day, they did their planning under the watchful eye of the very experienced Major de Koning, patiently guided by their IO.

When the moment came for them to pack up and move on to Pretoria for their final preparations, Jo-Jo felt that they had run out of time but Kokkie assured him there would still be time to brush up on techniques and emergency drills in Pretoria as well as in the operational area before deployment. All of them were so exhausted from the long hours of physical exertion and little sleep that they all fell asleep before the C-130 had even taxied out for take-off.

♦

Proper planning and preparation prevents piss-poor performance, goes the old British Army adage. Their so-called 7 Ps, which are briefly discussed in this chapter, are also applicable to the business world.

No Special Forces team would go on a mission without planning and rehearsing together. Business teams are expected to perform and deliver, sometimes without any proper planning, preparation or a favourable team environment. Business teams also need to plan and train for the goals they want to achieve. Once the right team is in place, the objectives are clear and the planning is completed, the execution almost becomes a formality.

 ## KEY LEARNING: PICK THE RIGHT PEOPLE!

In *Good to Great* Jim Collins writes, 'If we get the right people on the bus, the right people in the right seats and the wrong people off the bus, then we'll figure out how to take it someplace great.' It is critical to get the right team members for the job.

From the outset Captain Jo-Jo realises no individual possesses all the skills required but that each team member is an expert in his field of interest – a principle that would later greatly contribute to the success of the team. Da Silva is an explosive expert and has a knack for radio work; Steve's field of expertise is in medicine; Themo has excellent tactical skills and Jo-Jo is an outstanding leader, has sound knowledge of the area they are going to operate in and is a qualified forward air controller.

Simon Sinek said, 'We can't all be good at everything. This is partly the logic behind having a team in the first place, so each role can be filled with the person best suited for that role and together, every job and every strength is covered.'

One individual does not possess all the knowledge and skills to perform the tasks, which requires team members to depend on each other and work together to achieve the team's goals. Members have clear and distinct roles based on their area of specialisation. Knowing these strengths (and weaknesses) is critical when roles are defined or tasks are planned. Chapter 2 elaborated on the selection process and individual characteristics that can be used to select the right team members.

At this point Team Jo-Jo still has to prove itself as a well-coordinated and effective team but early indications are that Captain Brown has put together a formidable cast. It is now essential that the team members rehearse together to get to know each other's strengths and weaknesses and start working together as a well-oiled machine.

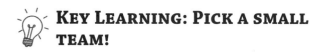 KEY LEARNING: PICK A SMALL TEAM!

Jo-Jo Brown had many reasons to believe a smaller team would have a greater chance at success than a big team. Given the aim of the mission, the need for clandestine infiltration and secrecy as well as effective communication out in the bush, he knew a team of no more than four men was required.

In the business world it is equally important to limit the size of the team to the smallest number of people which will be able to complete the project on time. Effective teams have as few members as necessary to perform the tasks.

Once a team goes above a certain size, problems of communication and coordination increase considerably. Rather consider breaking up a big project into different sub-projects and assign smaller teams to help complete it.

Even though Themo communicated through the use of hand signals, the message about a possible threat was immediately conveyed and the rest of the team could react. Team members must be able to communicate effectively with each other, not only to share information and give instructions but also to resolve conflict. Respect is built among team members when communication is open and direct.

The following two diagrams clearly illustrate the difference in the communication structure between a four-man team as opposed to a ten-man team.

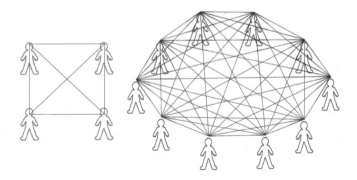

Not only does coordination become more difficult if the team size increases but a phenomenon called 'social loafing' also rears its head. What this comes down to is that the effort per team member decreases the bigger the team gets. The bigger number hides the effect of team members who don't fully perform but the effect is much more visible in a smaller team.

Effective teamwork means every team member participates and contributes to the success of the team. The mission of our team could have been compromised if Themo did not spot the hunter; even worse, the lives of the team members could have been at stake!

KEY LEARNING: PLAN TOGETHER!

No planning should be done without involving other team members and relevant departments. It is also important to acknowledge the expertise of all parties involved. Sadly, in companies the value of individual team members' contribution to the planning phase is often overlooked.

Very few company bosses or team leaders are experts in all the fields in which their team members excel. They also don't always have an exact idea of what the practical implications are of the work done by individual team members. Not only is there a real possibility that they could get unrealistic timelines but they also risk a low level of buy-in from team members, when in fact they require total commitment to the project goals.

Captain Jo-Jo did some informal planning with Da Silva who provided valuable input towards size of the team and selection of members. Detailed planning was then conducted with the team around their emergency plan and escape and evasion procedures. Jo-Jo also planned the mission in close cooperation with other colleagues and mentors – Kokkie, his boss, Thabo the IO and Det the signals Sergeant-major. To ensure he gained all information needed for the deployment, he liaised closely with the Air Force, the Military Health Service and MECSUP.

The planning process helps team members to better understand what is expected of them – this empowers them in an important way. In addition, they will feel more motivated to achieve the goals set out to them if they have been involved right from the start and perhaps even have had a say in formulating the goals. In this way, every team member buys in on the project which in turn leads to stronger commitment.

In Special Forces operations certain principles are applied during all stages of the mission: planning and preparation, deployment and lastly, execution and consolidation.

These stages can be compared with project stages in the business environment.

Irrespective of the methodology used, projects should, at a minimum, go through the following stages:

- ☐ initiation (budget planning, prioritisation of deliverables and justification for doing the project);
- ☐ planning (exploration of different options to achieve the project deliverables, project definition and planning);
- ☐ implementation and control (apply execution and control processes and allocated project resources and implement according to plan); and lastly
- ☐ closure (commence operations, handover, project closure and post implementation review to determine what worked well and what didn't).

 KEY LEARNING: REHEARSE TOGETHER!

Thanks to their rehearsals, Jo-Jo could immediately identify different remedial actions when the hunter was spotted. Our Special Forces Small Team conducted intensive rehearsals to hone their tactical skills, practise emergency drills and plan for contingencies. Radio procedures were meticulously tested and medical skills were fine-tuned with the simulated evacuation of wounded buddies from firefights.

The team spent a full day at MECSUP's facilities to familiarise themselves with the flares. At that point Captain Jo-Jo then realised that the flares were in fact quite potent explosive devices and consequently safety procedures were incorporated into the final rehearsals of the team.

While business teams should attempt to plan and train for every eventuality, it is not always possible from a time and cost perspective. It is therefore important to identify the key aspects that can go wrong. Then steps should be taken to ensure the objective will be reached and checks and balances then put in place to ensure the required outcome.

Rehearsals could mean the launch of a new product or service to a controlled group of people to monitor that all features are working, or simulating near-real situations. It could also be in the form of a team deploying new software from one test environment to another and testing whether the deployment procedures and functionality behave as expected before it is ultimately deployed into the production environment where real customers and organisational staff will use it.

The team leader could also pick a small deliverable and execute the approach to understand how well the team and the approach work, in order to make adjustments. Often during these rehearsals issues are identified and rectified that otherwise would have led to disastrous consequences during the execution.

In his book *Recce: Small team missions behind enemy*

lines, co-author Koos Stadler relates how they would experience a sense of déjà vu when stalking around in enemy bases – simply because they had studied the target so intensely and rehearsed the execution so well in exactly similar surroundings. They often had the surreal feeling that they had been there before. Similarly, if the team in the business environment encounter contingencies that they have rehearsed beforehand, they can respond quickly with the relevant remedial action and still achieve the objectives.

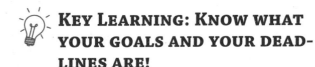

KEY LEARNING: KNOW WHAT YOUR GOALS AND YOUR DEADLINES ARE!

Everyone in the team needs to know what the goals of the project are and how this will aid the purpose of the organisation. Successful completion of a project requires that a specific set of tasks be executed in a specific order and within a specific time frame. These tasks should be identified during the planning phase.

In the military, a mission or task is conveyed through the so-called five Ws: Who must do What, Where, When and What thereafter? Once these elements are covered there should be no ambiguity regarding the nature of the task.

Team members should go to work with a cause and leave with a sense of achievement. This is not possible without clear direction broken down into goals. To make a meaningful difference they should work towards achieving these goals. Without tasks there are no milestones to be achieved. Reaching these milestones, big or small, should be celebrated as progress builds team cohesiveness. It also allows the leader to praise often but punish where it is due. When goals are achieved, the 'feel good' chemical dopamine is released in the brain's reward and pleasure centre. Dopamine enables us to see rewards and take action to achieve them. Never underestimate the power of progress!

Simon Sinek wrote, 'Dopamine is released when you accomplish something you set out to accomplish, when you cross something off your to-do list, when you hit the goal. Dopamine makes us achievement machines but we have to know that we're making progress.'

Victor remembers a recent project where a software development team was tasked with developing a new sales tool for a company. Three teams – a development, testing and business team – had to work together and ensure coordination to deliver the end goal. The goals and deadlines of one team were not necessarily aligned with the next team, which caused continuous delays, resulting in missed deadlines and low team morale due to not completing any significant deliverables. A few notable changes were implemented as to how the teams interacted with each other and communicated goals and deadlines across the teams. This ensured everyone was aligned and focused on the right tasks at the right time. The teams started ticking items off their to-do list and could see that they were making good progress. Within six weeks of the changes the teams achieved their end goal.

💡 KEY LEARNING: RECOGNISE AND REWARD TO MOTIVATE!

Employees, like all humans, have certain needs that have to be satisfied and there are certain factors that have an influence on their behaviour. Motivation theories like Abraham Maslow's hierarchy of needs and psychologist Friedrich Herzberg's two-factor model deal with these needs and the factors that influence behaviour.

Maslow's hierarchical order of human needs defines lower- and higher-order needs that must be met in a specific sequence. The assumption is that behaviour will be directed towards a need that is not met but once that need is met, then the behaviour will focus on the next need.

Physiological needs (salary, basic working conditions) and security needs (security in the workplace, job security, insurance, medical and pension schemes) are classified as lower-order needs and must be met first. Affiliation needs (friendship, acceptance, understanding by other people and groups), esteem needs (self-respect, recognition, success, appreciation) and self-actualisation needs (full development of individual potential, creativity, control, co-creation) are classified as higher-order needs.

Herzberg's two-factor model identifies factors that lead to work satisfaction which he calls motivator factors. The factors that lead to work dissatisfaction are called hygiene factors. Motivator factors are related to work content and positive feelings about an individual's work. These factors include achievement, recognition, work itself, responsibility and advancement.

Hygiene factors are related to the work environment and include organisation policy, supervision, salary, working conditions and interpersonal relationships. One of the key contributions of the model is that it points out that if organisations only focus on hygiene factors, motivation will not occur. Herzberg also classifies salary as a hygiene factor, theorising that people work to earn salaries but he also states that a monetary reward linked to performance classifies as a motivator factor.

Employees have basic needs that must be satisfied but they also want to advance their knowledge, have autonomy, achieve success and they want to be recognised and be rewarded for it. Dale Carnegie pointed out that 'people work for money but go the extra mile for praise, recognition and rewards'.

There are various ways to achieve the higher-order needs of Maslow or the motivator factors of Herzberg within a team context:

Give recognition in front of the group. The short interval control meeting described in Chapter 4 is a perfect place to acknowledge performance. These meetings give the team leader the opportunity to give recognition to a team member who has gone above and beyond his duties, displayed exceptional behaviour or achieved a task on time. Buying the whole team coffee and doughnuts will also go a long way.

Give greater responsibility and autonomy. Give people meaningful tasks to work on and if they meet the expectations; do not hesitate to give them tasks they have not done before. Provide guidance and then allow team members the freedom to complete tasks and make their own decisions.

Multiple examples throughout our story affirm this, such as when Jo-Jo delegated tasks to team members during planning and preparation and granted them the autonomy to make their own decisions.

Have regular one-on-ones. Schedule monthly 30-minute one-on-one discussion sessions between the leader and individual team members. Provide feedback during these sessions on positive and negative performance. It is important to provide specific feedback on how the team member can rectify negative performance. Understand failures and unpack the factors that contributed to them.

Share knowledge, a new technique or a different approach that can be implemented to make the tasks easier to complete. This will prevent the team member from attributing his failure to a lack of skill and knowledge, and will encourage him to try again.

Share key strategic information that team members would not necessarily receive via normal communication channels. Make a point of clarifying key information that was shared. Invite the team member to discuss topics that would not necessarily be discussed in the regular daily meetings. Get to know the person and talk about topics that are not work related.

Provide access to the inner circle. Create opportunities for team members to interact with senior managers and executives. Provide a team member with the opportunity to give informal or formal progress feedback to an executive sponsor or group. Prepare team members to have a discussion about a problem or a suggested approach with a senior person, or allow them to prepare and brief the team on tasks that must be executed. On the one hand, it will give them a sense of the pressure that goes with interacting with the inner circle; on the other it will make them feel that their inputs are valued. Kokkie prepared Jo-Jo for his briefing with the boss but he allowed him to make the presentation so that he could get the required exposure.

Create development opportunities. Look out for courses or conferences that individuals can attend to improve their skills or learn new techniques. If relevant, ask them to prepare a short overview and let them teach the team. It will increase their self-worth if the new technique is adopted as the new standard for the team. Create opportunities for everyone in the team to develop their leadership skills and send them on short leadership or coaching courses. This will benefit the individual, the team, as well as the organisation.

Reward the valence. Yes, give the medal *and* a cheque! Herzberg states that monetary reward can be both hygiene and motivator factors. Valence is the value or importance that an individual or a team attach to various work outcomes.

The premise of this book is centred on how the right individuals are selected to form the right team that is assigned to achieve a specific outcome. Highly applicable in this context is Stephen Covey's assertion that 'interdependent people combine their own efforts with the efforts of others to achieve their greatest success'.

To inspire team members to achieve even better

results, it is therefore important to provide for individual and team rewards and incentives. Michael Schrage, a research fellow at MIT Sloan School's Centre for Digital Business wrote, 'People need to feel that the benefits of being team players measurably outweigh the perceived and real costs of compromise and self-sacrifice. That's the incentive for taking incentives more seriously.

'Recognise and reward the firm's most dynamic duos and productive trios by name. Identify and celebrate the "fab fours" and creative quintets of innovation or efficiency. In other words, top management should seek out talented teams, not just gifted individuals.

'Teams, not just individuals, should get their fair share of bonus pools. A perceived – or real – absence of fairness can cripple team culture.'

KEY LEARNING: EARN TRUST!

In his movie *Up the Yangtze*, Yung Chang says, 'And without trust, you have nothing. Trust is the single most important factor in personal and professional relationships. It is the glue that holds people together … Trust comes from others only when you exemplify solid character.'

All teams go through a number of development stages before they become a performing team. It's in the inter-actions and experiences of people during these stages and once a team has become a performing team, that trust is earned. The 1965 Tuckman Model defined these stages as forming, storming, norming and performing.

A fifth stage called adjourning was added in the 1970s.

- [ ] **Forming** – Team members familiarise and form ground rules. Rules and regulations are maintained and members are generally treated as strangers.
- [ ] **Storming** – Team members are still very individualistic but they start to express their views and feelings. Team members fight control and show hostility towards leaders.
- [ ] **Norming** – Team members get a sense of belonging and realise that they can achieve goals better by working together and listening to each other.
- [ ] **Performing** – Team members start working in an environment of mutual trust where adaptability is the key and chain of command is recognised but not significant.
- [ ] During **adjourning** (at the end of the project) the team conducts a critical self-assessment to recognise members' contributions, celebrate successes and identify transition plans if required. Not all teams adjourn, some just move on to the next project and re-form. This stage has also been called the mourning stage in group development as some members may feel insecure or uncertain about the future, especially if the team is to be dissolved after the project.

Trust develops over the course of time during the relevant team-forming stages described above. Compassion with other team members, a belief in their competence and integrity are key ingredients for trust to develop. Trust builds a strong and effective team. It means that in times of need when you have to rely on fellow team members, you are safe in the knowledge that you can trust them and don't have to be concerned about personal attacks or being undermined by someone on the team. Instead, they can focus on their task with undivided attention.

Trustworthiness in business teams is earned when each team member consistently delivers what they have promised or were tasked with. Distrust forms when fellow team members do not meet these expectations, which in turn, leads to poor team performance, withholding of information by team members and, inadvertently, conflict. Teams need to develop and reach a stage where there is mutual trust before optimal performance can be obtained.

Our Special Forces team members have taken extraordinary trust to its highest level by taking 'a leap of faith' and literally putting their lives in each other's hands. The cost of one's trust being violated in the Special Forces context could well be fatal. In this context Rudyard Kipling's words become highly applicable: 'For the strength of the pack is the wolf and the strength of the wolf is the pack.'

Victor and his team were approached by a short-term insurance company to assist with the General Ledger

(GL) on a system that had not been designed correctly. It caused additional manual work which created opportunities for human failure during the month-end processing. The last straw was a negative correction that had to be made on the balance sheet due to these faults. The budget did not make provision for the extra loss.

The financial year-end was approaching and the company's executive did not want to go into the new financial year with the same issues. The managing director's instruction to Victor was clear, 'Get a team together, re-design the system, develop, test and implement it on 1 July when the next financial year starts and make sure the GLs balance.'

All of this had to be done in six months.

A small team of five people was put together. It consisted of a business analyst who specialised in accounting with extensive exposure to the system that was used, two developers who specialised in the financial module of the system, a tester who specialised in financial testing and a team leader who had good experience in these types of projects.

The tester and the business analyst had worked together before and knew each other well. The two developers also had a long working relationship and knew each other's strengths and weaknesses which made it easy to decide who would develop what.

The team leader had over 15 years' experience and was well regarded by her direct report. The team started planning together and the team leader made sure that there was clarity around the purpose, goals and direction. The planning also included other teams in the company.

When they considered the potential challenges, they identified the time constraint and the discrepancy between the test data they were working with and the company's real data. While the redesigned system might work with the test data, there was a real possibility that it might fail when the system was made live and the actual data was used. To counter this risk, it was decided to rehearse with a duplication of the actual production data and transactions.

A further complication was the fact that a new short-term insurance product also had to be tested and launched on the same redesigned system four days after the 1 July deadline.

The team started with the execution of the planned tasks. The development was completed four weeks before the 1 July deadline as planned, leaving only four weeks for the testing (normally you would need two months). The team knew that this was going to be tight and the team leader made sure that progress and issues were tracked and managed on a daily basis.

The high-level planning included testing the redesigned system in three phases. The plan for the testing phases went into extreme detail and had to be coordinated with other teams because the short-term insurance product also had to be tested on the redesigned system.

The first iteration of the testing went well and this motivated the team. The business subject matter expert got involved early on in the process (a contingency that the team had designed in) and approved the functionality so that the team could move the developed functionality to the next environment. Rehearsal 1 was completed!

The team prepared for rehearsal 2. Disaster struck! Some of the code that was supposed to be deployed did not move into the new environment. The team was devastated as time was not on their side. The cause of the failure pointed to a team member who didn't follow the deployment instructions for the redesigned system. These deployment instructions were updated and the team re-executed. Rehearsal 2 was a success!

They now prepared for rehearsal 3 which was done on the duplication of the real data. This had to be planned down to the hour as the new product had to be tested at the same time. This time the code was deployed successfully and the month-end test was executed.

The results were a cause for concern as the real data highlighted problems the test data did not reveal. However, the team was ready for any exceptions, so they quickly got together and resolved the issue.

On 30 June the system was tested a final time, passed and signed off at 19h01. It was ready for deployment on 1 July. The testing of the new product went according to plan and was successfully launched on 5 July!

A project generally involves a team of people – sometimes assisted by machines – specifically allocated to perform a particular task or achieve stipulated goals. The team makes use of material and financial resources and attempts to achieve value in terms of time, cost, performance, function and quality.

As we have seen, balancing and managing all these

factors can be quite complex and if not done correctly it will lead to failure. In summary, some of the key pitfalls which managers and team leaders should look out for and avoid are:

- ☐ **Lack of sufficient upfront planning**. Without proper planning, a team could start executing a project too soon and without a clear objective. This could also lead to them not doing proper project and risk management planning. This will have an impact on their efficiency and ability to reach the stated goal.
- ☐ **Lack of a properly defined implementation methodology**. Every project must go through the minimum four stages with a defined approach consisting of specific tasks to achieve the goals. The effort exerted on the project will only lead to re-work and waste if this is not in place.
- ☐ **Misalignment of expectations**. A project must result in positive changes to products or services and deliver on the expectations created to the stakeholders when it was initiated. Stakeholders can feel that the cost of the project exceeds the value it added if the expectations are not met.
- ☐ **Poor communication channels**. Be quick to listen but slow to speak. Listen to understand, not to respond. Guard against pre-conceived assumptions. The objectives of the project will

be at risk if the communication between team members and stakeholders is not effective.

- ☐ **Lack of executive support, management decision-making and ability to execute.** The notion in Chapter 1 that work teams form the DNA of organisations implies that members in the team share responsibility to make recommendations, implement their ideas and manage the outcome in order to achieve the organisation's objectives. The team should have the required authority and autonomy available to them to achieve the required objectives. The absence of capable leadership within the team and executive oversight that can make decisions to achieve the objectives will result in setbacks.
- ☐ **Lack of resources.** The team requires the right resources (machines, humans, materials and finances) in the right quantity at the right time.
- ☐ **Poor supply chain coordination (logistics).** The lack of proper logistics will result in resources not being secured on time, causing delays.
- ☐ **Failure to manoeuvre.** As the old saying goes, a battle plan only lasts until the first shot is fired. The inability to be flexible and adapt to change can cost a team dearly.

From team Jo-Jo's planning and preparations, a few key points stand out:

☐ Keep the size of the team as small as possible – only big enough to allow effective execution of the task.

☐ Get the right people with the right skills for the team – a key ingredient for success.

☐ Plan together – unleash the potential of each individual in the team!

☐ Rehearse together – develop a plan for each key contingency.

☐ Clarity of purpose and direction is important – everyone needs to know where they are going and why they are doing it.

☐ Reward and recognise teams and individuals.

☐ Trust is a must – teams can't operate effectively without trust.

4

INFILTRATION

An expectant silence settles down on the bush around the Special Forces team after the sun has set. Even the cicadas seem to be holding their breath.

At this hour sound carries far and any insignificant noise is easily magnified, so the team consisting of buddy pairs Jo-Jo Brown and José Da Silva on the one side of the hide and Themo Rodrigues and Steve Seloane on the other, remain in their positions, keeping absolutely still and listening out for any irregular sound. Apart from the occasional shouts of children and the distant bellowing of cattle from the village down in the valley that drifts up to them, all seems quiet.

Their mission is ingrained in each operator's mind: do a reconnaissance of the strategic enemy air base from where most air operations against own force are launched. Re-affirm the location of aircraft positions and enemy concentrations. Then set up specially designed flares that will be command-detonated by fighter-bombers on final approach. On completion of the aerial raid, the team has to remain in position on the high ground overlooking the target to assess damage and report on enemy reaction.

During the last scheduled radio call of the day, the tactical headquarters conveys a message that the execution has to be brought forward by two days. Apparently, this requirement was pushed by the Air Force because the attack needs to take place during the dark-moon phase.

Jo-Jo senses that something else must be at play, as there would be no moon in the early morning hours for the next two weeks. He doesn't even discuss it with the team; there was no chance he would risk his men's lives by steamrolling through the bush. He drafts a brief but firm response: 'Not possible. Execution as planned – Sunday morning.'

He receives no response from the tactical headquarters.

At last light, just before darkness completely engulfs the bush, team leader Jo-Jo gives an almost imperceptible whistle, the cue for everyone to start moving. Earlier, during the late-afternoon hours, all the operators had donned their anti-track booties – called 'elephant feet' due to the vague resemblance of the footprint to an elephant track – in preparation for the night's march. The purpose of the anti-track booties is not to imitate elephant feet but to mask the spoor sufficiently to deceive any would-be trackers.

The two buddy pairs start their routine to leave the hide and move into formation. Da Silva blends into the shadows of a tree and watches the darkening undergrowth, while Jo-Jo sits back into his pack and shifts the weight onto his shoulders by tilting his upper body forward. He gets onto his knees and, using some of the saplings around him, starts to erase all signs of his presence. First he levels the soil where his body and boots have left imprints, then he sprinkles a thin layer of dust over the area and, finally, he lifts the flattened grass sprouts around his position into their original shapes.

Holding on to the trunk of a tree and taking care not to leave any imprint in the sand with the stock of his AKM, Jo-Jo gets up and slowly moves to the edge of their hide, facing in the direction he knows their compass bearing would take them. Da Silva goes through the same procedure to get his pack on, also ensuring that no imprints are left where he prepared the radio antenna.

Jo-Jo opens his compass and finds the bearing he inserted earlier. The stars are already clear in the night sky and he soon locates one low on the horizon to fix his bearing on. By the time he is ready to move, Themo, the indomitable scout, is in position in front of him, glancing back to check that his team leader has noticed him.

No hand signal is needed, no re-checking of kit – the team has rehearsed this routine over and over again and know it by heart. Quietly the formation moves out, each operator vigilantly covering his allocated arc of responsibility and taking care not to follow directly in the tracks of the operator in front of him.

While there is no moon during the first half of the night, the stars are bright and the ambient light is sufficient for them to identify a route through the undergrowth, taking care not to leave any tracks.

The packs are heavy and the going is tough. They move at a snail's pace as each man has to carefully pick his own route within the formation, concentrate to leave no sign and stop frequently to observe.

Even though the night is relatively cool, Jo-Jo is constantly thinking of their water consumption. He decides to ease the pace and calls a halt after barely one kilometre.

Their only water replenishment point is still two days away – and there is no guarantee that they will be able to access the water source which was also used by the local population.

The team takes a 15-minute break. They move out again before their muscles stiffen. Soon they settle into their patrol routine, covering stretches of one and a half kilometres and resting for no more than 15 minutes at a time. By 03:00 Jo-Jo realises their fatigue has been slowing them down and that they need to settle for the day ahead. They have covered a solid 12 kilometres. During the next break he instructs Themo to look out for a hiding place for the coming day.

After they have settled down on a rocky outcrop, Jo-Jo walks away from the team and out of the circle of all-round defence to act as listening post but not before he ensures that Themo, who is nearest to him, has been made aware of his movement. Once his ears become attuned to their surroundings he realises how much noise there is – crickets, the odd jackal, the wind through the leaves, tree frogs, occasionally an owl … and was that a rifle shot in the distance?

He briefly recalls how quiet it was after they had landed the night they parachuted in. The utter silence and sense of complete desolation were so overwhelming that he was momentarily immobilised. But there was no time to waste, as the team had to regroup, discard the parachutes and establish a cache with the emergency water and rations before daylight.

During the planning phase they had debated the pros

and cons of freefall parachuting versus a static-line jump at length. This was an important decision, as it would determine the choice of aircraft as well as the altitude they would jump from. For static-line jumping, where the parachute is attached to the aircraft and actually opens on exit, a low-level jump is possible. Freefall jumping, however, is done from a higher altitude and the freefaller opens the parachute at the time he selects.

Jo-Jo's preference was to be inserted by helicopter as it was by far the safest option for the operators. As opposed to parachuting in and landing on an unmanned drop zone, a helicopter insertion meant that they would land on a predetermined landing zone. Helicopters also had the added advantage of flying nap-of-the-earth, which meant that the aircraft remained below the enemy's radar coverage, thus reducing the chances of being picked up.

However, due to the vast distance to the drop-off point in southern Angola a helicopter insertion was not feasible. Even with maximum additional fuel tanks the Pumas would not have had sufficient reserves should there be an emergency; it simply did not carry enough fuel to take evasive action or circle back on an alternative route.

After lengthy deliberations with the Air Force liaison officer, they had decided on a static-line jump, mainly because the overall risk was lower. While they were all freefall qualified, landing with the high-speed freefall chutes on an unmanned and unmarked DZ in the dark of night would have been extremely dangerous.

For static-line parachuting the aircraft could also approach below radar coverage. On final approach to the

DZ, it would pitch to the jump altitude of 300 metres above ground level to release the jumpers – and descend for a low-altitude escape once the parachutists had cleared the aircraft. Another advantage of a static-line parachute jump was that they would have better control over the additional equipment that would be delivered by cargo chute.

Jo-Jo clearly remembers the severe tension of that night – the fear of parachuting onto a 'blind' DZ, the uncertainty of whether his men would be injured or would even survive the jump. After the landing, when he was lying there, he was momentarily paralysed, afraid to move for fear of discovering injuries. The fading of the C-130's sound in the distance only added to his intense awareness of the silence.

Then came the sudden impulse to move, to check that everyone was okay and the kit was intact.

The DZ was an open floodplain of a river southwest of the town of Chibia. Their biggest fear was that they would miss the open field and land in the trees along the edge of the floodplain. Since he had been the first one to land, Jo-Jo knew that he had to move in the direction of the aircraft's flight path to find the others. The moon was in its last-quarter phase and bright enough for him to find the rest of the team easily.

No one was injured and the cargo landed intact. It took them the rest of the night to dispose of the parachutes and cache the reserve equipment. For the parachutes four separate holes had to be dug, then the chutes stuffed in and the contents of a tube of chemicals poured over them. The holes had to be left open for 20 minutes for the chemicals to take effect properly.

They made good use of this time to carry the reserve equipment away from the area and cache the items in separate holes. By the time they were done, morning had broken and daylight was approaching fast.

They had moved a few hundred metres up the slope of the high ground spanning the river line and found a good hide to observe from. Making use of the early-morning light, Jo-Jo and Themo had gone back to check that the cache had been properly camouflaged and no tracks had been left. The parachutes would be completely destroyed by now and the chemicals would prevent any predators from digging up any evidence of their landing.

Jo-Jo had used the rest of the morning to map out the position of the cache on a sketch map, drawing in main features and distances, and had applied a simple code to indicate which items were in each hole. He had then visited each of the team members to ensure that they knew the exact location of the cache and would be able to identify the outstanding terrain features.

The team spends the entire day in their hide on the rocky outcrop. Not being able to move or even speak to each other puts enormous psychological strain on them. It takes immense effort to remain focused for 12 hours and not buckle under the uncertainty and stress that come with operating covertly behind enemy lines.

Fortunately all of them have completed extensive programmes to motivate themselves during extended periods of stress and isolation. As part of their advanced re-

connaissance course, *Special Forces psychologists teach the operators how to apply various techniques aimed at coping with the demands of the job. One exercise entails listing all the external factors that could negatively influence one's state of mind during a deployment, ranging from family issues to fear of death. The operator has to place all these negative reflections into an imaginary glass tube, dubbed 'the brain' and taint the tube with a colour he has a negative association with.*

In the next step the person lists a number of positive factors such as the fact that they were selected from thousands of candidates, had done extensive training comparable with the best in the world, were physically fit and capable and were well nourished, healthy and highly motivated. The operator acknowledges these points and accepts that each one of them is applicable to him.

In the final step he groups all the positive factors together and paints them with a colour that he has a positive association with. At this point he has to drain the negative factors from 'the brain' by slowly pouring the positive colour in until it is only filled with constructive thoughts.

It is a simple exercise and one they had to do repeatedly during the course but Jo-Jo found it very helpful. He had applied it before and also during every subsequent operation.

To deal with the boredom, Jo-Jo has worked out a simple but effective daily routine he strictly adheres to. After catching up on some much-needed sleep during the morning, he first studies the map and memorises their route, noting all possible obstacles and laying-up points and studying available escape routes, emergency RVs and possible pick-up points. Then he brews some coffee and takes his time to enjoy it with a granola rusk. He savours every bite; after all, time is on his side and there is no one rushing him.

After that he visits each team member, not only to confirm the coming night's route and the emergency RV for the day but also to give them a short pep talk. Back in his position he prepares the day's message on the data entry terminal.

Lunch, while simple, is one of the main events of the day and therefore an elaborate business. He boils some water on his gas stove to which he'll add a packet of freeze-dried chicken biryani. Once it's done, he'll eat it slowly, savouring each bite to turn this humble meal into an enjoyable affair. During the long and drawn-out afternoon hours, he reads his Bible and tries to memorise a verse.

At some point Da Silva, having already prepared the radio and antenna, will collect the data entry terminal from him and establish comms with the tactical headquarters, dispatch the message and receive one from the HQ for Jo-Jo's attention. If necessary he will respond to it. In the late afternoon he again visits each team member to confirm the route as well as the emergency RV for the coming night, taking time to motivate them, share a joke or just chat for a few minutes. He is relieved to find everyone in good spirits and ready for the task.

Two nights later they reach the valley where they intend to replenish water. They observe the area for a whole day *from an observation point on the southern side. The well is a hub of activity as the villagers bring their herds of cattle and goats to quench their thirst. This has one advantage – the team's tracks will not be noticed, especially if they remove their shoes and apply strict spoor discipline.*

During that afternoon's scheduled radio call Jo-Jo receives an unexpected and somewhat alarming message. They are tasked with planting a flare at each apron – where the fighters are parked on both ends of the runway – instead of at the western perimeter of the base.

'Air Force needs targets to be marked for precision bombing. Report on feasibility once visual on target,' the brief message states. It ends with the following note from the general officer commanding: 'Your safety is priority. Only execute if deemed possible. Execution confirmed for Sunday morning.'

This changes the dynamics of the whole deployment because now they have no option but to penetrate the base. Jo-Jo imagines how, when the Air Force did its own rehearsals, the pilots concluded that the targets need to be literally highlighted for an effective assault at night. Weighing up their options given their team size, Jo-Jo discusses the request with Da Silva before he calls the other two for a brief planning session.

They sit in a tight circle opposite each other, each covering the back of the buddy in front. Jo-Jo runs them through the change in plan and explains the implications. They will have to split up and execute the tasks separately, one team inside the base and the other on the bombers' run-in to the west.

Themo immediately wants to know who will be penetrating the base to plant the flares. He doesn't wait for an answer before telling them he believes he is the best man for the job. Their discussion soon turns into an argument, albeit in muffled tones. Jo-Jo calms the men down and asks them to disperse; he will do the detailed planning and inform them who will be doing what in due course.

Later that night they approach the water well, having slept during the first half of the night. Now, in the early-morning hours, they use the last weak light of the waning moon to replenish water. Jo-Jo sends two team members at a time as the water has to be pulled up in a bucket and poured separately into each water container. It is a time-consuming process because they have to work quietly and fill the containers one by one. As each operator has at least 40 litres to replenish, it takes the better part of two hours for the four men to complete the task.

By sunrise they are well away from the valley but now discover that the populated area, which mainly consists of maize fields interspersed with small settlements, stretches for kilometres towards the target area. Most of the vegetation has been removed to make way for crops. Jo-Jo realises that they will be in trouble if caught in the open fields; so they have no other option but to find a hide before the villagers arrive to work in the fields.

Finally, they stumble upon a small cluster of shrubs under a few trees. Each buddy pair moves into a separate position and caches their rucksacks close by. They then settle in head to foot, on their backs, and prepare for the long day ahead. Jo-Jo takes care to cover Themo and

Steve up with twigs and dried leaves, ensuring they blend in completely with the undergrowth.

Then he moves in next to Da Silva, who has removed the radio in its runaway bag from the big pack to keep it next to him. They sit facing each other as they camouflage each other's legs, then lie down on their webbing, which has been loosened slightly and pulled up to serve as elevation for the head. This way they can cover 180 degrees towards their buddy's back.

The day's rations consist of two Tarzan bars (energy bars designed to contain the nutrients of a full meal) and nuts. Water is taken through a tube running from a water bag attached to the webbing. It is broad daylight; now they dare not move.

As the day drags on, people can be heard working in the fields around them. Occasionally a shot is fired, sometimes uncomfortably close by but Jo-Jo assumes it is the Militia, a kind of citizen's force responsible for local protection and intelligence gathering among the communities.

Fear is an ever-present companion and can only be mastered if one understands the processes the mind goes through and learns how to cope with it through deliberate countermeasures. All people experience fear but the ability to contain it and continue with the task at hand is a skill very few have mastered.

The day becomes a long, drawn-out and frightening one during which no member of the team can afford to relax, even for the briefest moment. Their nerves are frayed and sleeping is out of the question, as they know that they can be discovered any moment.

Only by late afternoon the activities start to subside as the workers begin to head back to their dwellings. Finally, as the sun sets behind the trees and calm is restored to the bush, the team crawls out of their hiding places.

Jo-Jo allows 20 minutes for stretching and eating. Then they don their anti-tracking booties and by the time darkness has engulfed them, they are on their way.

The going is slow, as they now have to take extra care not to leave prints or disturb the bush. They take three hours to cover the three kilometres to the edge of the high ground overlooking the enemy air force base and nearby town. Jo-Jo decides to let the team rest for the remainder of the night to ensure they are fresh and rested in the morning. The bush is relatively dense on the edge of the plateau and he is certain they will find a suitable observation post during the first few minutes of daylight.

♦

 ## KEY LEARNING: TRAIN FOR MENTAL RESILIENCE!

In his book *Legacy: What the All Blacks can teach us about the business of life*, James Kerr writes, 'Bad decisions are not made through a lack of skill or innate judgement; they are made because of an inability to handle pressure at the pivotal moment.'

Jo-Jo learned this valuable lesson from the encounter with Sixpack Stevens during the selection course in the

Caprivi. To escape capture was not about running through the bush as fast as possible but about mastering the pressure brought on by the situation and having a clear mind to take the appropriate measures to achieve success.

Whenever tasks must be completed within certain deadlines, you will find stress. Stress can be triggered by a variety of stimuli and people have different reactions to it. These reactions can be affective – where individuals feel anxiety, tension, depression – or cognitive, where they experience a sense of helplessness or difficulty in making decisions. People can also have a physical reaction to stress in the forms of a headache, nausea, or gastric-intestinal disorders. Another reaction is behavioural – impulsivity, hyperactivity; and motivational – loss of enthusiasm, disillusionment, demoralisation.

Our Special Forces team knew they would experience many different kinds of stress on their mission. They operated deep into enemy territory and if they were caught they could be killed. Apart from that, executing their mission was also extremely dangerous and had to be completed within a specific time frame.

Fear was a constant companion for the team members, especially when they had to wait for hours on end in their hide. Fortunately, they had been trained to have the mental resilience to face this fear. During their selection course survival instructor Ray Templeton helped to develop their mental resilience when he took away their shoes despite the sand being too hot to walk on and when he made them lie for hours in ambush under the scorching sun. They simply had to find a way to overcome this physical challenge. They were also taught how to apply a coping mechanism to deal with fear by colouring their negative thoughts and draining them from their 'brain', replacing them with positive thoughts.

Stress reactions present themselves differently at the individual, interpersonal and organisational level. It can have disastrous effects on team members, deliverables and progress.

Kerr also identified two states of mind individuals can have, namely Red Head and Blue Head. A Red Head is tight, inhibited, results-oriented, anxious, aggressive, over-compensating and desperate. A Blue Head is loose, expressive, in the moment, calm, clear, accurate and on task.

In a Read Head the amygdala, which is the part in the brain responsible for the response to emotions especially fear, hijacks the brain which will cause a person to either fight, flee, freeze or appease. In a Blue Head the prefrontal cortex, which is the part of the brain involved in complex planning, coordination, decision-making and executive function, opens up and the person has access to empathy, judgement, higher decision-making and innovative capabilities.

The ideal is for all team members to be Blue Heads. Numerous interventions are available to help avoid stress reactions in the work environment and to assist team members to stay in the moment, be calm and on task and make clear and accurate decisions:

☐ Break big deliverables up into smaller tasks. This will make the workload more bearable and assist with better scheduling to ensure that the smaller tasks don't overlap or compete with each other.

☐ Improve communication and decision-making in the team. Identify and discuss issues constructively. Allow the team to make decisions. If the team does not have the autonomy to make decisions, make sure the relevant structures are in place to assist the team with decisions they can't make. This will ensure a constant delivery rate of deliverables.

☐ 'Know yourself'. With greater self-awareness team members will be able to identify signs and symptoms of distress. They mustn't be discouraged by numerous failures. They need to stay calm and focused. This will allow them to remain open to possible solutions and make rational decisions.

☐ Coping skills can be developed to deal with stress. Developing these coping skills and gaining experience in managing stress at work will assist individuals in overcoming similar situations in the future when they have to face them.

 ## KEY LEARNING: TIE UP LOOSE ENDS!

A significant lesson can be learned from the way in which the team cached their reserve equipment and buried the parachutes after landing. Each member took responsibility for the task of stowing away kit, destroying evidence and restoring the area to its original form.

In organisations it is paramount that, as sub-objectives of a project are concluded and the team positions itself for the next phase, loose ends from the previous phase are tied up. All unfinished tasks should be concluded, outstanding problems addressed and mistakes noted.

On one of Victor's projects a team had to transfer short-term insurance policies electronically from an old system to a new system. The majority of the policies were transferred successfully but a small subset had to be done manually due to missing data which meant clients had to be contacted personally for the outstanding information.

A key part of the automated process was that the old policies were automatically cancelled once the transfer to the new system was successful. However, for the policies that had to be transferred manually, the cancellations had to be done manually.

The euphoria of the successful migration of the majority of the policies caused the team to slip up on the task to check that the manually transferred policies were also cancelled. These policies were all double debited at the end of the month which resulted in a few very unhappy customers.

KEY LEARNING: MAINTAIN THE AIM!

Everyone in a team needs to work towards achieving the end goal. Team members must be engaged and they need to know what they must do on a daily, sometimes hourly basis. Aligning the focus of all team members on the overall goal and maintaining the aim, will lead to high-performing teams.

In their hide, Jo-Jo took time to visit each team member during the infiltration to confirm the coming night's route as well as the emergency RV for the day. He made an effort to reinforce the night's objectives and keep every team member engaged. Re-affirming the emergency RV helped to instil confidence in each.

Once they moved out, they maintained their focus and diligently covered the distance they had to travel to reach the target area on time.

Maintaining the aim on a mission or a project requires discipline from both team leaders and members, especially when seemingly small, incremental changes creep in. In such instances it is important to ask whether the change contributes to the main aim as it could influence team deliverables. A seemingly insignificant additional task may eventually escalate and demand more capacity and energy (dependencies), which in turn may affect the initial aim.

Soon the team ends up with dependencies that were not planned for and resources that are not available when they are required which will inevitably lead to delays in achieving the goals.

When he received the radio message asking them to move the execution forward by two days, Jo-Jo assessed the risk to the team and to the success of the mission before informing his superiors that they would not be able to change their plans. Decisive leadership is a critical success factor in a small team environment. It is incumbent on team leaders to make the final decision and ensure that the team's objectives are achieved. If this requires the leader to challenge the wisdom of his superiors, so be it; being unpopular sometimes comes with the territory!

Shortly after new software was implemented at a short-term insurance company the employees were asked to identify how the system could be improved, or enhanced. These enhancements had to be prioritised.

During the release of a part of the enhanced software one of the business analysts added a small requirement onto the list of priorities without discussing it with the team leader. The development team assumed this requirement would form part of the final list of items that would be released and didn't question it.

Testing continued as per plan. A while later the team leader realised there was a discrepancy between the items on her list and that of the development team. The unauthorised item, although small in terms of development time needed, required substantial testing and the people who had to do it were tied up with the other items on the deployment list. The item created a dependency!

The dependency on the human resources was one problem, while an additional problem was that the development team had configured the software code in such a way that the entire software release was jeopardised if the item was not tested in time.

The team leader assessed the situation and requested

input from the team regarding available options. She made the call to remove the item from the deployment list. This cost the team dearly as they had to stop the project, wait two days for the specific software code to be removed and then start the testing from the beginning.

The team missed the original planned deployment date, albeit by only a few days, because the business analyst didn't have the discipline to say no and didn't maintain the aim. Thanks to the team leader, who forced the team to refocus and return to the original aim, the project could be salvaged.

Having the discipline to say no to extra tasks that will not necessarily contribute to the agreed goals will ensure that the focus is maintained; saying yes may often destroy that focus. Team leaders play a particularly important role as they often have to stand by the courage of their convictions and say no when the situation demands it.

As Stephen R. Covey wrote, 'You have to decide what your highest priorities are and have the courage – pleasantly, smilingly, unapologetically – to say no to other things.'

 ## KEY LEARNING: ASSESS THE RISK!

While Jo-Jo and his team were considering the options for their infiltration – either freefall parachuting, static-line jumping or helicopter insertion – the pros and cons of each had to be evaluated and the risks weighed against each other. In consultation with the Air Force's liaison officer they opted for a static-line parachute infiltration –

it was less risky than a freefall insertion but potentially much more dangerous than a helicopter landing.

Chapter 3 mentioned a lack of sufficient upfront planning as one of the reasons why projects fail, especially due to a lack of proper risk assessment. Although the stakes are much higher in the Special Forces environment as lives are at risk, businesses have similar stakes where key projects can be delayed, costing the company in additional capital expenditure or in lost revenue, which could jeopardise the wellbeing of the company as a whole.

Therefore, potential risks should be determined at each key step of a project so the right choices can be made and the end goal can be achieved. The assessment of the risks or the consideration of alternatives should be a collaborative approach which must involve the team leader, team members and other relevant parties.

In the business world, Victor has also seen the sad results of a lack of risk assessment. In one instance a big food manufacturing plant had a critical piece of machinery as part of their production line. If this piece of machinery broke the whole plant would come to a complete standstill, costing the company millions of rands.

Although the machine was highly reliable, one part of the machine was notorious for breaking. This part could only be imported from abroad and usually took four weeks to arrive.

While the part was expensive, it was still less than the financial loss of four weeks of lost production. Victor therefore recommended that the maintenance manager keep one spare part in stock in case the machine broke down.

The maintenance manager ignored the advice, saying, 'The machine never breaks down and we don't have the budget to purchase a spare part now.'

A few weeks later the machine did indeed break, costing the company dearly. This could have been avoided if the maintenance manager had done a proper risk assessment.

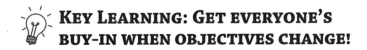 KEY LEARNING: GET EVERYONE'S BUY-IN WHEN OBJECTIVES CHANGE!

Often project goals change or are adjusted. When goals are amended, team leaders should ensure that everyone in the team is on board. If the plan changes, the team has to discuss and jointly agree on how to achieve the new outcome.

To get team members' buy-in on a new strategy or end goal, ask for their input. When Jo-Jo received the radio message tasking them with the extra responsibility of planting a flare at each apron, he discussed this development with Da Silva and then called the other two team members for a brief planning session to get everyone's input before making a final decision.

In some Special Forces outfits, the powerful, face-to-face and brutally frank sessions referred to as 'Chinese parliaments' are used to get maximum input from all team members and sometimes make life-and-death decisions.

People feel respected and valued if they are included in decision-making, even if only partially. It will be much easier for a new strategy or goal to be adopted if the people who are about to execute the task have a say in how it will be done, or at least what they think about the plan.

It cultivates a culture where team members feel free to question the status quo and think for themselves rather than simply do as they are told. It also creates an opportunity for a team leader to get multiple inputs, to show that she is willing to listen, that members' inputs are valued and that she is mature enough to adopt a potentially better suggestion.

KEY LEARNING: TAKE OWNERSHIP!

Taking ownership of a project means that team members identify so closely with the aim of a project that it becomes a personal responsibility – it starts with each team member and ends with the team leader. It also means taking responsibility for all the tasks that were allocated during the planning phase and knowing that each person will be held accountable for all decisions and results, regardless of whether the project is a success or a failure.

In our Special Forces team each member took ownership of their arc of responsibility, camouflaging the position of the hide and taking caution not to leave any tracks or signs of their presence. Each team member knew that he could put the team at risk by not taking the necessary safety precautions. Consequently, everyone worked towards this goal.

When the achievement of the aim becomes the

individual's absolute priority, no sacrifice is too great and no hardship insurmountable. The team experienced great uncertainty and severe stress when they inched their way towards the target through densely populated areas under enemy control. What kept them going was that each of them had taken ownership of a shared goal.

A scorecard helps to ensure that team members continue to take ownership for a project. Peter Drucker, an American management consultant and leader in the development of management education, said, 'You can't manage what you can't measure.'

A scorecard system is a simple but effective measure to understand responsibilities and account for progress. Making the scorecard visual and tracking progress in short interval controls to ensure everyone knows the score at all times are key elements to determine progress.

The scorecard should consist of a collection of goals derived from the strategic objectives that are to be achieved by the team. These goals must have specific measures and targets that will make it easy to track each member's and the team's progress. It should cover the full extent of accountability for each member or the team as a whole.

It is also important that the scorecard contains lead and lag measures. Lag measures reflect whether or not you have achieved your goals, while lead measures indicate the likelihood of achieving the goals. Lead measures drive the attainment of lag measures. Team members should therefore learn to focus on the lead measures which they can still influence, and not on lag measures.

An effective way to address progress, or lack thereof, on

a regular basis is to use the short interval control method. This is a factory-floor process that is used to drive production attainment. Short interval control can take place in the form of a stand-up meeting, a coffee-conference, a Chinese parliament session or a team huddle.

At a practical level, short interval control comes down to a series of short (15- to 30-minute) focused reviews, carried out every day by the team to review progress and to identify actions that must be taken to improve performance in the future. The core principle behind the method is very simple: we cannot change the past (lag measures), however, we can learn from them to improve the future (lead measures).

During the planning, Jo-Jo divided the distances more or less equally between the nights to create a measure to track progress and ensure they arrived at the target on time. He visited each team member late in the afternoon to confirm the emergency rendezvous and the route that had to be accomplished during the night's march.

During each short interval control review the team should take the existing plan with allocated tasks and address a series of steps under the following two headings:

Looking back on recently completed tasks:

- ☐ Which tasks were supposed to be completed?
- ☐ Were these tasks completed?
- ☐ If so, assess previous actions and evaluate their effectiveness and whether follow-on actions are needed.
- ☐ Team leader to give credit where it is due.

☐ Team leader to give constructive feedback where required.

Looking ahead to next tasks:
☐ Identify future tasks from the plan, confirm and accept responsibility for tasks.
☐ Identify upcoming conditions and changes that may adversely affect the completion of the tasks.
☐ Decide on a specific set of actions to be completed to ensure the tasks are completed successfully and the risks identified are mitigated.
☐ The actions decided upon during the short interval control review are then carried out by the team to maximise progress.

Knowing your goals and sticking to your deadlines are two vital elements in taking ownership. This will also ensure that a member earns the trust of other team members. Individuals who repeatedly don't do what they have committed to or miss deadlines, will not only cause distrust among team members but will also cause poor team performance.

Team leaders must take ownership of the team's performance and each team member must take responsibility for their own performance. Individuals must have the conviction to stand up in the short interval control progress meetings and account for the lead and lag measures that they own.

Taking ownership often requires a team leader to make difficult decisions. This can entail correcting a team member or standing up to management if she believes an instruction will have a negative impact on the team's performance or the achievement of the end goal.

Given his experience and his assessment of the situation on the ground, Jo-Jo realised he would be endangering his team if he agreed to move the date for the attack on the air force base forward. Consequently, he informed his officers that he couldn't accept their command. When the Special Forces team was tasked to plant flares inside the base, there was some disagreement when Themo pushed himself forward as the best candidate to do so. Again Jo-Jo took control of the situation and told the team he would make the final decision after getting everyone's input.

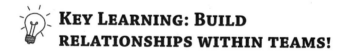

KEY LEARNING: BUILD RELATIONSHIPS WITHIN TEAMS!

It is important to build strong relationships among team members but it is even more important for team leaders to build solid relationships with their team members. This leads to a feeling of connectedness and emotional attachment among team members and between the team leader and team members. Jo-Jo sealed this bond with his fellow team members by visiting each of them, taking time to check on their wellbeing and trying to inspire them.

In this trust is a key ingredient. Team members will give everything when there is connectedness and a sense of emotional attachment to others and the team leaders but their performance will be merely mediocre when this is absent.

It is important for a team leader to have an understanding of what his team members are feeling and thinking. Good relationships are best built through face-to-face interaction. Personal contact instead of e-mail or telephonic conversations needs to be encouraged. Make an effort to meet team members and ask for their input and opinions, hear their concerns and try to understand what they are experiencing in the team context.

This is applicable to all types of teams, including management teams. Victor experienced a feeling of non-connectedness and emotional detachment in an incident involving the managing director, or team leader of the management team, of the consultancy firm he worked for. One of the partners, or management team members, raised a serious concern that was shared by most team members. While all the partners were shareholders, the managing director owned 70% of the shares.

Victor's partner said that while he respected the fact that the managing director took the risk to start the company and was grateful that he allowed the other partners to purchase shares, he felt they were treated unfairly. 'We helped to grow this company from a revenue income of R10 million to R50 million over the years, yet the majority of the dividends go to one individual. We simply don't bear the fruit of our efforts. We need to find a way to correct this, or I will have to leave the company.'

The response from the managing director was as

follows: 'I hear you but can we not discuss this at the next director's meeting in four weeks?'

In this instance the managing director did not connect with the concern, get what the other shareholders were experiencing or hear what they had to say. All the shareholders left within 12 months.

Team members will also look out for each other when they are emotionally attached and connected to each other. Our Special Forces team members were concerned for each other and made sure that everyone was properly camouflaged when they lay up in their hide during the day.

On one of Victor's projects a Muslim team member was involved in a car accident. Since his car had to go in for repairs and he had no other means of transport, he could not attend mosque on Fridays, as was his custom. The team leader noted how the situation was affecting him personally and offered the use of his vehicle on Fridays until the team member's car was fixed. The team leader connected with this member of his team and understood that going to mosque was important to him.

When the two happened to meet each other ten years later, the team member's first words to his wife were, 'This is the guy I told you about who was willing to give me his car to go to mosque!'

By looking out for the team member, the team leader left a lasting impression and created a willingness to walk the extra mile.

While it won't always be possible to get involved on

such a level, the point is that one should acknowledge your team members' humanity and not only think of them as just employees. Team leaders who are truly able to connect with their team members and display empathy, are bound to be respected and trusted.

 KEY LEARNING: COOPERATE ON ALL LEVELS TO WIN!

Successful teams cooperate well with other teams, both internally and externally. The aim of the interactions between teams should be to advocate the common purpose, build consensus, share knowledge, discover common opportunities and agree to support each other. It is about cooperating and achieving overall group success instead of giving in to individual domination, egoistic behaviour and personal gain. Extraordinary things are possible if people coordinate.

Our Special Forces team also had to work closely with other teams, in particular the Air Force, to ensure their parachute jump would be executed successfully. In turn, the Air Force depended on the team to have the flares positioned correctly for the bombing raid to be effective.

Where more than one team is working on a project, cooperation should happen on a macro level. A core team may often be dependent on deliverables from other teams to achieve their end goal.

For example, in an organisation a process and system-design team may need to work closely with the product-design team, while both teams may have to work with the system-development team in order to get a new product to market.

In another example from the business world, a process and system-design team headed by Victor was busy implementing new software. It was developed by a systems development team from a company in a city 500 kilometres away. The two teams had worked very closely together and united in their commitment to complete the project on time and on budget.

On the go-live day after the process and systems-design team had done all their checks, Victor agreed that everyone could call it a day and go home. The module in the system that calculated the monthly or annual premiums of a policy was extensively tested before the implementation, so no extensive checks were performed again.

The only check that would still be done was to ensure that the module did return a premium when the correct information was captured. A team member in Victor's team who was responsible for the premium testing stayed behind and decided to run one test case. He discovered that something must have gone wrong during the implementation as one of the premiums calculated at a tariff of 1.5% instead of 15%. Everyone, besides him and Victor had already left!

Victor could not get hold of the development team to resolve the issue. It was important for everyone to achieve a successful go-live on time, so he called the director of development from the company who had supplied the software and explained his predicament. The director was at a very important function but immediately excused himself for 20 minutes, fetched his laptop from his vehicle and corrected the issue himself.

Over the preceding months, a strong relationship had developed between Victor and this director. This relationship of trust, together with the shared common purpose to go live, enabled this cooperation.

Building cross-functional relationships (relationships across teams inside and outside the organisation) is therefore key to team success. If the leader and team members can interact and influence other teams to see a cooperative goal and understand that they are in the same boat, rowing towards the same shore, they will soon realise that they need to work together.

The team either wins together, or loses together. The company either achieves its goals, or it doesn't!

Building a network of relationships with internal and external stakeholders is an important building block to achieve cooperation on all levels and across teams. A good strategy is to get a number of trusted team members to collectively advocate the goals to key members in supporting teams so that the whole group will rally around a common purpose.

Influence is the capacity or power to get people's cooperation without forcing them. John C. Maxwell, an American author of leadership books, wrote, 'Leadership is influence.' It involves connecting to people by listening to them and finding common ground; showing people how both parties have the same needs and want the same outcome, and how they share the same values and concerns.

Once a collective purpose has been inspired, a sense of interdependency between teams will develop. Again, trust is a prerequisite for building strong relationships. Reciprocity now starts to play a role as team members will learn to help others in return for their assistance. Individuals will reciprocate and cooperate if they feel valued and cared for.

A team at a financial services company had to develop, test and deploy four major consecutive software releases. The releases contained new functionality and defect fixes in the existing software that was used to sell new policies, administer existing ones and process claims from customers. The releases had to be done in a very short space of time.

The challenge was that the software releases had to be implemented during the latter part of the year after the team already had a taxing year behind them. Furthermore, it had to be completed before 1 December when system freeze would start (no software releases are allowed from this date to ensure system stability).

The team started planning together and developed a high-level plan with the following deadlines:

- ☐ Release date 1: 3 August
- ☐ Release date 2: 31 August
- ☐ Release date 3: 7 September for system functionality and 8 September for policy migration

(the transfer of policies from the old to the
new system)
☐ Release date 4: 16 November

The release manager ensured that everyone knew exactly
what had to be done in each release. This informed the detailed development and test planning as the team had no
time to plan after each release. A release would move into
production on the planned date and the very next day at
09:00 the next release would be in and testing had to start.

There were several requests from individuals in the
business that the software releases should include additional functions but the release manager diligently guarded
against these being added. This was because these extra
items could cause code dependencies and one item could
delay a whole release if it could not be tested in time.

It was important to work closely with teams from other
business units using the software as they had to conduct the
final testing and sign-off before the new software could be
installed and used by them. The release manager made a big
effort to share the plan with the other business units and
make sure that the relevant resources were informed and
available when required to do the testing.

The employees who were using the software were
also asked for input on the plan. The high-level plan
was shared with them and they were made aware of the
important role they were playing in ensuring the releases
were delivered on time.

The plan was visualised on a scoreboard and every
team and individual knew what they were responsible

for and by when. Releases 1 and 2 went well and according to plan. Release 3 included the release of a new product that enabled another team to migrate policies from the old to the new system that incorporated this specific product. The scheduled date for the release was 7 September.

However, the project team did not receive the code on time from the development team to start testing. This caused the testing time to be shortened as the deployment date of 7 September had to be stuck to for the scheduled policy migration to take place on 8 September (sufficient time had to be allowed for the policy documents to be generated and delivered on time and within the legislated period by 15 September).

Every morning the team met for 30 minutes in front of their scoreboard to discuss progress, problems and action items for the day and more importantly, to make decisions together. The team discussed the issue of the delayed deployment and the release manager asked for input from team members.

One team member came up with a suggestion that would allow for certain testing tasks to be conducted together but it deviated from the standard operating procedure. The team discussed the risks and the release manager decided to accept the plan. The plan was executed and the team made good progress.

But then disaster struck! A day before the planned software release Group IT informed the team that they had to shut down all the computer servers on 8 and 9 September for emergency maintenance due to constant ransomware attacks. The software release could be done on 7 September but the migration team would miss their migration objective as they would only be able to start on 10 September!

Again the team came together and discussed the challenges and decided to move the deployment date to 11 September and the migration date to 12 September. This required some cooperation from the people in the company who were using the software as the policy document generation had to be done both during the day and at night to meet the deadline of 15 September. The policy document generation for migrated policies is usually only done at night due to the negative impact it has on the performance of the software if done during the day while everyone is using it.

Everyone understood the dilemma of having to generate the documents during the day and knew that they were in the same boat as customers would complain if the documents were not done on time, so all agreed.

The deployment was executed on 11 September and the migration of the policies took place the next day. The documents were all generated and e-mailed by close of business on 15 September.

The team did not waste any time and started with the testing of Release 4. People using the software approached the project team because they had an issue. They were behind schedule with a business project they started and needed a change in the software to minimise the impact on customers. A request was made to consider an interim release before Release 4, to change a restriction on the software and extend it by another year.

The team got together and looked at the viability and the impact. The team also had to reciprocate as the assistance by the other business units contributed significantly to their delivering on time. The estimated development time was limited to two days but since major testing had to be done, one of the key resources for Release 4 would not be available.

The team started making plans and cooperated with the actuarial team to assist. The plan was finalised and executed. The interim release was deployed on time with minimal impact on Release 4.

Constant requests were received for additional items to be added to Release 4. The team diligently evaluated the risks and in the words of Stephen R. Covey, pleasantly, smilingly and unapologetically said no to the items that could possibly impact the delivery date of Release 4.

Release 4 was delivered on 16 November!

In summary, a few key points:

- ☐ Through continuous training and self-improvement, train the brain to be a Blue Head!
- ☐ Engage team members; make sure everyone knows exactly what they need to take responsibility for. Visualise it. Own it.
- ☐ Keep focus on your original objectives, get buy-in from everyone if the objectives change and have the discipline to say no to additional tasks.

☐ Take the time to assess risks and tie up loose ends to increase the probability of success.

☐ Measure performance in regular short intervals and manage it!

☐ Build relationships, both inside the team and with external partners. Find ways to influence external parties and get them to cooperate to achieve your goals. Then reciprocate!

5

EXECUTION

At first light they wake up with the sound of fighter jets taking off in rapid succession. The sound lasts for a steady ten minutes and Jo-Jo makes a mental note, as it will impact greatly on the success of the mission if all the aircraft are not on the ground during the bombing raid. It is still too dark to identify the planes taking off but a quick calculation tells him that no less than 20 fighters have taken to the skies.

By sunrise, they have settled in among a cluster of rocks on the edge of the plateau. Another long day of silence and no movement awaits them, having established an observation post (OP) directly above a spread of enemy positions around the air base below. They also know that during the night they have passed an enemy radar position on the plateau where a company-strength protection element was stationed. The protection force was sure to patrol the area surrounding the radar station.

They observe the target for two full days. The OP offers a limited view on the air field but at least they have clear sight of aircraft taking off along the eastern tip of the runway. Da Silva meticulously records every aircraft taking off, steadily building up a picture of the air traffic involved in the war zone. On both mornings the fighter jets depart just after first light and return in pairs about 40 minutes later. Da Silva dispatches the data by DET to the tactical headquarters and receives a thumbs-up from Special Forces head-quarters; the information is significant as it indicates that the aircraft are on the ground during the night. It also means that the bombing raid needs to take place before any air-craft takes off at first light. The go-ahead is given for the team to penetrate the base on the second night and for the raid to follow at 04:00 the next morning – a tight schedule, as it leaves no margin for error. Once the flares have been planted, the team has to be out of the danger zone before the bombers arrive.

They make their move before sunset of the second day in the observation post. They steal a bit of daylight since their time schedule is extremely tight, having to penetrate and execute the task before 02:00 – and be back in the OP by the time the air strike comes in at 04:00. After the air strike, they have one day to remain in the OP and assess the result of the attack. Another consideration is that their water will last them only two more days, leaving a very small margin for E&E. Jo-Jo makes sure that the emergency RV is known to everyone – the very rocky outcrop that has served as their hide and OP the past two days. They cache their packs among the rocks and take only the smaller bags designed for carrying the flares.

During the long hours of the day Jo-Jo has been plan-ning the execution in minute detail. He has divided the team in two: he and Da Silva will penetrate the base from the west and plant the two flares at the aprons, while Themo and Steve will take care of the flare on the bombers' run-in, 1000 metres to the west. When he conveyed his plan to Steve and Themo, they'd had a stormy disagreement –

albeit in muffled tones – as Themo did not want to hear anything about the choice. Finally Jo-Jo had to put his foot down. 'Guys,' he said, 'one team inside, one team outside, finish and klaar. We cannot have two teams penetrating. We need a foot on the ground outside. And besides, it is too dangerous to have two teams inside. What if things go wrong and you start shooting at your own comrades?'

Themo didn't like it and wanted to know why they could not penetrate while Jo-Jo and Da Silva plant the flare on run-in. But the decision was final. In the end Jo-Jo had to throw in a witty remark to lessen the dread, 'Because I say so. And because I navigate better than you. And because I don't have a wife and kids who will make your life miserable when I'm dead.'

They agreed that Themo will take the radio in its runaway bag and Steve will keep the first aid pack with him. Once the two of them have executed, they will move back to the OP, set up HF comms with the tactical headquarters and keep a listening watch on the VHF radio while they wait for the other team to return. By 03:30 they will all be listening out for the incoming bombers. Once comms has been established with the lead pilot, Jo-Jo will give the go-ahead code word, 'Black Forest'. If anything has gone wrong and the bombing is to be called off, a repeated 'Red Shirt, Red Shirt, Red Shirt' will be the code to abandon, upon which the aircraft will return home immediately.

Jo-Jo and Da Silva have also donned their stalking gear – moccasins, tight-fitting woollen knee and elbow covers, balaclavas and night-vision goggles with specially designed harnesses. Each has strapped a two-litre water *bag to his webbing. Each one also carries a flare with the receiving device in bags specially designed to remove and set up the flare with the least amount of effort.*

The two teams descend down the slope and move in a north-westerly direction to their planned dispersal point to the west of the target area. Their map appreciation has indicated that they would encounter the least amount of obstacles around the western edge of the base but first they have to circumvent a platoon-sized enemy post in a cluster of bluegum trees at the bottom of the escarpment. All along they have been aware of the position and have observed the activities from their OP but still take great care to avoid it. Their task is made easier by loud music and drunken singing from the cluster of trees; it is Saturday night and obviously party time!

Once past the enemy base, they reach the tar road running from the air force base in a westerly direction. It is only eight o'clock and Jo-Jo takes a moment to orientate everyone. He picks a cluster of trees just south of the road as their crash RV – in case of an emergency on target. Everyone acknowledges the point and they move out after a brief rest.

At the pre-arranged dispersal point west of the base they split up. There are no elaborate goodbyes, just a pat on the shoulder and then Themo and Steve disappear into the night in the direction they have to plant their flare. Jo-Jo and Da Silva wait until the other two have gone and the night has turned completely silent. After listening out for a few minutes, they start their approach.

From the western perimeter, it is only a 300-metre stalk to the first apron where the one group of fighters are parked. An approach from the west would mean that they stalk against the prevailing wind. Since the moon is now in its dark phase, they do not have to consider the effect of moonlight during the stalk. An unexpected aid is the music drifting in from the platoon base now southeast of them; it gives them a firm reference point for navigation and helps to mask any noise they might make.

They soon reach the perimeter – a sturdy chain-link fence three metres in height, flanked by cleared pathways both inside and out. As planned, they take up a listening post in the brush on the side of the path. Their patience is soon rewarded, as within ten minutes they hear a foot patrol approaching from the south.

The discipline is poor and the patrol tactics almost non-existent, as the team can hear the patrol approaching from more than 50 metres away, bantering and joking among themselves. From their position close to the ground, the team can see the four guards against the ambient light of the night sky as they pass within a few metres. Weapons are slung and they all seem to be relaxed.

As soon as they have passed, Jo-Jo nudges Da Silva and indicates that they should move. The fence has to be cut and signs covered up before the next patrol arrives – within the next 50 to 60 minutes, according to their observations. Da Silva wastes no time; he leaves his flare pack with Jo-Jo and moves out to the fence, gloves on, wire cutter ready and two sizeable pieces of thick cloth handy. While using the cloth on both sides of the cutter to muffle the noise, he starts clipping the chain link piece by piece, a routine he has practised to near perfection. Jo-Jo listens into the night, ready to call his buddy back at a moment's notice. He observes his surroundings and mentally registers two tall trees that would mark their exit.

Within minutes Da Silva has cut a wide half-circle that he now pulls aside like a trapdoor. Jo-Jo passes his pack on and then stoops to wipe any tracks they might have made with a small branch. Once both are inside, Jo-Jo moves into the low vegetation while Da Silva bends the fence back into position and ties in a few ends to make it stay in position. No one will notice the disturbance in the darkness.

Jo-Jo leads the way. He has mastered the art of DR, short for 'dead reckoning', a technique where compass bearing and exact distance are used to do pinpoint navigation in featureless terrain. He has complete confidence in his navigation skills, having applied this exact type of precision-navigation countless times before and he knows that they will hit their intended mark within a few metres.

Suddenly the far-away but clearly distinguishable 'thud' of an explosion directly from behind them in a due westerly direction, reaches their ears. They stop in their tracks. As they turn around, the amber glow of a bright light source is visible above the horizon.

'You're thinking what I'm thinking?' Da Silva whispers into Jo-Jo's ear, his voice trembling ever so slightly.

'Could be,' Jo-Jo whispers, 'but there's nothing we can do about it now. We are almost there ...'

Crouching low, they maintain a slow but steady pace towards the apron. It is just after midnight when they reach the tarmac 15 minutes later. They go down on their bellies, now even more vigilant as they know that the enemy has a tendency to position guards under the dark frames of their aircraft.

They observe for ten minutes and are soon reward-ed when a faint light appears, moving steadily around on the apron in front of them. Jo-Jo quickly realises that the person with the light is moving around on the tarmac be-tween aircraft positions or guard posts. Once he is sure that the light-bearing person maintains a routine on the hardstand in front of them, he crawls up to Da Silva and indicates that he is going to plant his flare while his buddy keeps a lookout.

They have spent endless hours practising this part. Set-ting up the flare and arming it should take no more than two minutes. But suddenly a dreadful feeling has come over him: what if the explosion they have heard and the amber glow they have seen barely 30 minutes ago was in-deed the other team's flare that has malfunctioned?

From his training years before, Jo-Jo forces himself to drain the negative thoughts and fill his consciousness with positive ones. They have rehearsed this over and over. He has personally checked the mechanism and has ensured that the self-destruct timer was set on six hours. The pro-cedure was easy, the chances of error zero … almost.

Once the flare has been set in position and crudely cam-ouflaged with dried twigs and grass, Jo-Jo connects the wire to the VHF receiver and switches both devices on, then commences with the arming procedure. After he has pulled the pin, he finds himself sweating and his heart pumping but he maintains enough presence of mind to put the pin in his breast pocket – as proof that the flare was armed.

They move out immediately, Jo-Jo still leading the way. The northern end of the runway is virtually clear of deployments and infrastructure – and would offer covered escape routes if the team was compromised. By moving on the edge of the runway, they make good time without leaving any disturbance or making even the faintest noise. They reach the apron on the eastern end within 25 minutes, leaving them with enough time to execute and still backtrack on their infiltration route.

Da Silva expertly removes his pack and starts preparing the flare while Jo-Jo covers. Da Silva positions the device just off the tarmac within 30 metres of the first aircraft. They have not located any movement among the planes but it is too dark to distinguish any shapes and they know that guards would be lurking somewhere among the parked fighters.

A diesel engine starts up, then a search light pierces the night sky barely 200 metres from their position. Now they can hear shouting in the distance towards the terminal buildings; vehicles are being shunted and doors are slamming – a search party being mobilised? Something has happened to stir things up. Flashlights have been switched on and are moving among the aircraft – too close for comfort.

Da Silva is undeterred. He goes through the arming procedure, scouts around briefly to see that Jo-Jo is away from the flare and pulls the pin. He moves off to join his team leader. Together they slip across the runway and into the low brush on the northern edge.

More search lights have joined the spectacle and are

crisscrossing the dark skies. The team keeps a low profile but makes good time in the low undergrowth. By 1:30 they reach the western end of the runway. The last 300 metres to the perimeter requires spot-on navigation, as there is no time to cut another hole in the fence; scaling the top would be too dangerous. Jo-Jo checks his compass and finds a star on the horizon to fix his bearing on. The noise from the base in the bluegum trees has subsided. Only the distant roaring of vehicles in the direction of the terminal buildings reaches their ears. The stretch to the fence takes them a painstakingly slow ten minutes as they now have to be exceptionally vigilant; if the guards have been alerted, the perimeter would definitely be guarded.

They have almost reached the fence when a vehicle suddenly approaches from the south, driving slowly and shining a searchlight into the bush on the far side of the fence. The team goes down into the grass. But the soldiers are clearly more concerned about a threat from outside and seem to take no notice of their immediate surroundings inside the fence.

Then the vehicle stops. Jo-Jo's heart misses a beat as he immediately suspects that they have found the hole in the fence. There is some loud talking, doors are slammed and then the vehicle continues along its path. From the nervous voices of two or three men, the team gathers that soldiers have been dropped off along the fence.

As soon as the vehicle has passed, Jo-Jo finds his bearing and stalks forward, Da Silva following closely. They reach the road at the exact point where the fence has been cut, the two trees that they noted during the penetration clearly visible against the night sky. They can hear the soldiers who have been dropped off, chatting in subdued voices about 30 or 40 metres to their left but consider them a minor hassle – as long as there is no light.

Jo-Jo motions to Da Silva to go. The big man slips across the pathway and opens their gateway in less than five seconds, then indicates to Jo-Jo with a slight click of the tongue to follow. Once Jo-Jo is through, Da Silva bends the fence back in position and ties it in, then bends down and covers their spoor with a branch he has plugged from a bush.

Da Silva leads the way as they move into the undergrowth, swiftly getting away from the fence in case the vehicle with the searchlight returns. Once clear of the perimeter, both switch on their VHF radios, knowing that they urgently need to get comms with Themo and await the call from the approaching bombers. Using Steve's call sign, Jo-Jo calls into the handset every few minutes, 'Sierra, Sierra, this is Juliet,' but receives no response. He stops and signals for Da Silva to wait.

'We have to decide, are we moving back to the OP or to the point where the flare was set up?' he whispers. But before Da Silva can answer, the handset crackles and Themo's voice comes across,

'Juliet, Juliet, this is Tango. Problem. Problem!' From his high-pitched and panting voice, Jo-Jo can detect the anxiety. The fact that he speaks openly and doesn't use their pre-arranged code for distress indicates to them that things are not well.

'Tango, this is Juliet, are you both okay?' he asks.

'Sierra not okay. Wounded in the face. Cannot see,' the dreaded answer comes.

'Where are you? Jo-Jo wants to know more but he realises this is not the time to try and extract further details.

'Crash RV. Crash RV ...'

'Stay put. I say again, stay where you are. We are coming to you,' Jo-Jo assures him.

They start off at a trot but Jo-Jo realises that the enemy will probably find the hole in the fence and attempt to follow their tracks from there. It is crucial not to leave a trail. Time has suddenly become a critical factor. It is now 3 o'clock; within the next hour the air raid will come in. If Steve is in a bad way, they may have to call off the strike.

♦

KEY LEARNING: DEVELOP A TEAM CODE OF CONDUCT!

Some of the best teams in the world – Google, Apple, US Navy Seals, British SAS and the All Black Rugby team, to name but a few – have a set of principles they live by and that inspire everything they do on a daily basis. The principles function as their code of conduct. It sets the baseline for behaviour and acts as a reference tool that helps team members to understand what is expected of them.

This set of principles should be written down and must be placed where it is visible to all. It is important to develop the code of conduct together and ensure that everyone agrees to the principles.

Each small team should develop its own, unique culture or *esprit de corps* that should be based on the norms of the group, unique vocabulary used and practices followed, the metaphors used by team members and the rituals observed by them. It can be visually represented in a logo or emblem.

The power of an *esprit de corps* should not be underestimated. It creates an environment that can inspire people, give them a sense of pride and enable them to flourish. A team with high morale is more likely to walk the extra mile and will be far more resilient when recovering from setbacks than one with low morale. High morale is built up over time as the culture manifests in the team and trust among team members increases.

If a team has a clear and visible code of conduct, team members can also be held accountable if they violate it. It makes it easier to address an offender and repeat offenders can be asked to leave the team.

As mentioned in Chapter 1, our Special Forces team also had a set of nine principles they operated by. These nine principles can also be applied in the team environment in different organisations.

- ☐ **Outstanding leadership:** Transformational leadership – that is, leadership that is visionary and inspiring. To achieve harmony, the team leader should lead as if he were a conductor up front, at the podium of an orchestra of individual players.
- ☐ **Cooperation:** Individual effort is always in support of the team's objectives; every member

works towards a single goal.

- ☐ **Mutual support:** Although each team member performs as an individual, everyone is willing to step in when another needs assistance. With mutual support a team can be synchronised.
- ☐ **Know each other's strength and weaknesses:** Team members and team leaders should know how each team member performs under different circumstances. If you know a team member can be relied upon even under stressful conditions, it helps to build trust.
- ☐ **Plan together:** No planning should be done without involving all team members and acknowledging their expertise.
- ☐ **Make decisions together:** Frank face-to-face sessions (the 'Chinese parliament' principle) should be used to get maximum input from all team members.
- ☐ **Maintain the aim:** All team members should work towards achieving the end goal. Objectives can only be changed or adjusted when the entire team concurs.
- ☐ **Commitment – a firm belief in the cause:** Goes with the characteristics of dedication and taking ownership but here *the team* has made that solemn pledge.
- ☐ **Rehearsals:** Rehearse for every contingency – this is a critical principle to ensure success of the mission.

Adhering to these principles helped Special Forces teams to develop an *esprit de corps* and be successful in their missions. Jo-Jo displayed outstanding leadership right from the start.

He selected a small, competent team and then guided them through the planning and rehearsals. At certain points he allowed other team members to take the lead and gave them the relevant authority to make decisions.

The briefing he provided during warning orders was concise and clear and he made sure everyone understood what was required of them. He made firm decisions during the mission, took time to talk to the team members and motivate them.

The team planned and rehearsed together until the plan was perfected and everyone knew exactly what they were responsible for and by when; then they committed to make the mission a success. They made decisions together when the details of the mission changed. Some of these were made based on the strengths and weaknesses of individuals.

They maintained the aim of the mission, focused on the execution and did not accept changes or additional tasks that could jeopardise the main objective. Cooperation and mutual support between the team members and other teams played a fundamental role before and during the mission.

KEY LEARNING: LEARN THE ART OF EXECUTION!

A focus on how to execute the task at hand should be a core part of every team's culture. There are many examples in the military and in the business world where a poor plan was saved by good execution and conversely, where a good plan failed due to poor execution.

In previous chapters, we discussed a few prerequisites that have to be in place before execution of a project can start. Firstly, the right sized team with the right team members must be selected. Secondly, everyone in the team must understand the project goals and how it furthers the purpose of the organisation. Thirdly, team members must have planned and rehearsed together and understand what they as a team and as individual members are responsible for. Lastly, they must have taken ownership and created a scoreboard to track progress.

Once these are in place, execution becomes almost a formality.

In *The Art of War* Sun Tzu writes, 'There are not more than five musical notes, yet the combinations of these five give rise to more melodies than can ever be heard. There are not more than five primary colours, yet in combination they produce more hues than can ever been seen. There are not more than five cardinal tastes, yet combinations of them yield more flavours than can ever be tasted.'

Just as the combinations of musical notes, colours and cardinal tastes create magic, teams can also create magic by combining five execution essentials that we'll discuss below.

Get started. Great ideas are just that – ideas! They are worthless if not implemented. Lao Tzu said, 'The thousand mile journey begins with one step …' If you want to go somewhere, you have to start walking; if you want to achieve your goals, you have to start executing.

Our team got into the C130 aircraft, hooked up their static lines and jumped out of the plane to start their execution. The sooner a team starts with that first activity on the plan, the sooner they get to the last one. It is better to get going rather than not mobilise at all. It is also better to fail while trying rather than not try at all.

Empower at the point of impact. Trust those in the trenches because they are closer to the situation and can take the best action. As General Norman Schwarzkopf, commander-in-chief of the allied forces in the First Gulf War once said, 'Even though higher HQ screws it up every way you can possibly screw it up, it is the initiative and valour on the part of small unit leadership that will win for you every time.'

When tactical headquarters changed the way the task had to be executed, they trusted Jo-Jo and his team to make the right decision once they had assessed the situation at the enemy air base. A team should have the authority and autonomy to accelerate decision-making and achieve the required objectives. A team with the right levels of autonomy who can make decisions stands a much better chance of making progress. If this is not the case, decisions will just be referred up the chain of command, leading to delays.

Leaders must be reminded that passing down this level of authority is done without giving up ultimate responsibility!

The following five steps can serve as a guideline for a leader who finds himself in a position where an important or difficult decision has to be made:

☐ Think – think through the problem/task/situation on your own;

☐ Outline – delineate the problem and ask team members for their suggestions and opinions. Stimulate participation and new ideas but otherwise keep quiet and listen attentively and open-mindedly;

☐ Discuss – analyse, evaluate and prioritise the different options;

☐ Decide – make the final decision and explain your reasoning;

☐ Implement – ensure that the decision is effectively implemented.

Exercise discipline. To execute a project demands discipline. The short interval controls should be executed religiously to track progress against the lead and lag measures on the scorecard. This, in turn, will allow the team leader to take the appropriate actions, including holding team members accountable. These short interval controls come in handy when the plan has to be changed and the team has to agree on the method and the actions needed to execute it.

Now it becomes important for team members to communicate well, coordinate and cooperate closely and guard against accepting tasks that can distract the focus and cause the team to miss deliverables. Jo-Jo and the team were the quintessence of discipline. They exercised extreme discipline, even under duress and this contributed significantly to the success of the mission.

Keep a Blue Head. It is easy to stay calm and keep a Blue Head when things are going according to plan. It is not that easy when the going gets tough, when the project timelines start slipping, when the budget is overspent and when poor quality impacts deliverables.

The body language used and the way someone communicates, especially a person in a position of authority, has the potential to generate unnecessary fear or uncertainty among team members. Epictetus, the Greek philosopher, once said, 'Circumstances do not make the man. They merely reveal him to himself.'

It is important for team leaders to stay the course, to remain positive and lead with courage.

When Jo-Jo and Da Silva heard the thud of the explosion and saw the amber glow of a bright light source on the horizon, they realised that Steve and Themo might have been in trouble. However, they chose to drain the negative thoughts, stay calm and execute their task.

Uncontrolled fear scares away success; fear that is controlled and directed towards obtaining the objective may add to the success.

Do the unexpected. When the enemy started suspecting something and launched a perimeter search, they were more worried about a threat from outside the base than inside. They probably didn't expect anyone to have the audacity to breach the perimeter fence and enter a strategic air base 180 kilometres into enemy country.

Three key elements were always present at the execution stage of Special Forces operations, namely surprise, purpose and stealth. These elements, combined with the principles of Special Forces operations like authorisation at the highest level and decision-making at the lowest, relatively small numbers and well-trained and highly motivated personnel tasked with a specific mission, contributed significantly to the successes that were achieved by the small teams of the reconnaissance regiments.

In business today, the element of surprise is induced by a combination of proficiency and stealth. If an organisation has a team that must deliver a breakthrough change that will give them an edge over the competition, proficiency and stealth can be a game changer. Unexpected action allows a company to develop and deliver a product to the market unexpectedly, which will enable them to gain the required market share. This can deliver a blow to competitors that they may struggle to recover from.

Exploit company strengths and competitor weaknesses. Have the audacity to do things in a way that was unimaginable before.

When one of the world's largest producers of pure, selenium-free, electrolytic manganese metal had efficiency issues, they contacted Victor's management consulting company for assistance. The company supplies electrolytic manganese metal to niche markets such as high-quality producers of aluminium, steel, non-ferrous alloys, electronics, chemicals and welding consumables.

It receives manganese-bearing ore from the Northern Cape as its primary raw material. The ore is milled and calcined at high temperature before the manganese metal is leached into solution. The solution is then purified and the metal is plated onto stainless-steel cathodes in a 58 kilo-amp (kA) cell-house.

The managing director was clear about what should be achieved: 'Increase throughput and reduce the ore and power requirements per ton of metal produced, more specifically, 83 tons of electrolytic manganese metal per day at 58kA with 70% low sulphur content.'

When Victor did a reconnaissance of the site he realised there was much mistrust of and hostility toward consultants. One employee who walked passed Victor didn't mince his words, 'You look like a typical consultant, are you here to f*ck things up further?' This was due to a previous consulting company who tried to achieve the same goals but failed. In the process members of the staff and the management team were alienated.

This mistrust could negatively impact implementation of the project.

Something had to be done to get everyone on board. Workshops were conducted to prepare the workforce for the forthcoming changes and to make the purpose and direction of the company clear to everyone – from the person knocking off the metal from the stainless-steel cathodes to the managing director. Employees across teams were rallied behind a common purpose.

An illustration was created to visualise where the company was going. The intention was to convey, through images, the company strategy and how to achieve it. This was shared with everyone during the workshops.

A holistic plant capacity review was required to understand and identify bottlenecks in the process.

Although the information required to do this review was available, it was largely fragmented and distributed among key personnel.

All involved parties had to collaborate to draw a sound conclusion and reach consensus regarding the key issues affecting product quality and plant capacity. Small task teams across sales, production and engineering were identified and put in place to start with the planning and the execution.

The small task teams received training and were coached in a more performance-based approach to managing teams. It involved a methodology that ensured that the right people discuss the right things at the right time and in the right way to get the desired results. The methodology made used of short interval control meetings, or Chinese parliaments, on a daily basis where the relevant teams got together to discuss progress.

A code of conduct was developed collectively and everyone had to pledge their commitment to the principles. The principles and illustrations that depicted the company strategy, were re-enforced during these meetings.

The members of these teams were all experienced specialists. Some of the team members had worked together before but some were new. A fair amount of storming, forming and norming followed before the teams worked well together.

A positive team culture started to develop, morale changed for the better and the same employee who was initially quite antagonistic about the intervention rallied behind the cause. In the end he became a key contributor to the process of finding solutions to ensure greater efficiency in the company.

An in-depth assessment of the management systems and processes, as well as the chemical manufacturing process capacity and product quality was conducted. Following an in-depth three-month review, a roadmap (detailed plan) for change was compiled by the relevant teams and presented for approval to management and the shareholders. The plan was authorised at the highest level and authorisation was given to the teams to make the relevant decisions and choices to ensure the objectives would be achieved.

The right people and teams were in place; they knew what to focus on and what to do and the team morale was high! It was time to execute.

Implementation followed a collaborative approach by leveraging on-site expertise structured into task teams. Over the next seven months, the task teams, which included members from Victor's company, diligently executed the plan and maintained the aim to achieve the goals set by the managing director.

The engineering team applied maintenance and reliability engineering principles which increased the time that the equipment in the plant was available for production. Breakdowns decreased and the tons started to increase!

The production team focused on critical-to-quality parameters. They had to ensure that the quality and quantity of the relevant materials used were consistent. This was to ensure that the required product quality (below 0.034% sulphur) and quantity (83 tons) could be repeated on a daily basis. Controlling these parameters was critical as rehearsals were out of the question due to the costs involved.

The team identified the critical-to-quality parameters that had to be controlled. They designed and developed process control charts (charts with upper and lower control limits) with the relevant actions that needed to be taken if the process started to get out of control. The team members were trained on these charts and the actions required to rectify the process when it started going outside the control limits. This required extreme discipline and the stress that came with the adjust-wait-and-see approach caused a few tense moments. But soon the product quality and quantity started to improve!

Achievement of the stated objectives was tracked by means of a benefits tracking model, illustrating the monetary progression of the implementation. The net effect was an annual saving of 3,6% of the total cost base. During the course of the project, a 4,3% increase in production output was achieved in relation to the base-line output. The net result exceeded the budgeted benefits! The company consistently started to produce 83 tons of electrolytic manganese metal per day at 58kA with 70% low sulphur content.

Now it was the task of the sales team to ensure the sales targets were achieved. Unexpectedly, the sales team, together with the production team, tried a new technique where they aligned production and sales requirements with electricity tariffs and foreign exchange rates. This introduced further cost savings and revenue generation.

In this chapter, a few key points stand out:

☐ Discuss the code of conduct within the team on a regular basis. Personally address team members who have not followed the code and recognise those who have behaved in the desired way.

☐ Create an *esprit de corps* and let it flourish. The organisation will be rewarded in the most unexpected ways. As the German writer and poet Goethe famously said, 'In comradeship is danger countered best.' Allow comradeship to become the vehicle that carries the team to success.

☐ Make sure the prerequisites for successful execution are in place, then create magic through the five execution essentials:
  * Start executing
  * Empower at the point of impact
  * Exercise discipline
  * Keep a Blue Head
  * Do the unexpected

6

EVASION AND EXFILTRATION

Jo-Jo and Da Silva make good time, now taking care to move silently and to leave no tracks. By 03:20 they approach the crash RV. Themo has switched on his infrared strobe and Jo-Jo picks up the flashing light with his night vision goggles from a distance. Jo-Jo warns Themo on the radio that they are moving in. They exchange passwords in hushed tones and Themo welcomes them into the hide.

Steve is sitting curled up against a tree. He is badly burnt, mainly on his hands, face and upper body. While he has no eyesight, he can still walk, albeit with difficulty. Themo has had to half-carry him all the way from the site of the incident to the crash RV.

'What happened?' Jo-Jo asks.

'As he pulled the pin the flare exploded. I was watching the area with my back to him, so I did not see exactly what happened,' Themo explains.

Jo-Jo sits down next to Steve and talks quietly into his ear. Steve's first reaction is to apologise, 'Sorry, boss. I'm so sorry …'

'It's not your fault, Steve. It's the equipment. Come on, we'll get you out of here.'

He takes a few moments to comfort his friend and then calls the other two to shield them off while he uses his torch to assess the extent of the wounds. Steve is in a lot of pain but Jo-Jo realises his injuries are not life-threatening and that Steve will manage to move if guided along. While he will not be able to carry any equipment, the insides of his hands are relatively unhurt and he can at least hold onto someone and carry light objects.

Their situation calls for quick decisions. The job has to be completed. Within half an hour the bombers will be coming in. At the same time Steve has to be moved out of the danger zone to an area where the enemy will not immediately search. The team needs food and water, however, if they are to survive the coming days while they evade the enemy and move away from the target area.

Heads close together, they confer. Jo-Jo's first concern is whether any equipment has been left at the explosion site but Themo assures him that he did a thorough check after he tended to Steve; only the debris of the flare remained behind. Their personal equipment, the HF radio and the medical pack have all been retrieved. A quick stocktake reveals that they have six litres of water among them, as well as emergency rations to last them at least two days.

'Okay, here's the deal,' Jo-Jo whispers, 'we have to get out of here. Soon this place is gonna be busted. We can't all go back to the OP; it's too dangerous. We'll leave a highway through the bush and they will surely search the high ground. But we need to get food and water, also the other HF. So we have to split up. The bombers are on their way, so I need to get to the OP. The question is, where is the safest place to take Steve?'

Da Silva's suggestion is that they move north around the air base where the enemy will least expect them to be but Themo counters that time is against them; also, Steve will not be able to anti-track so they'll leave a trail.

'The tar road …' Steve suddenly interrupts. 'Get me to the tar road.'

Jo-Jo realises that he has been focusing on the completion of the job so much that he did not see the obvious solution.

'That's it! Great Steve! Da Silva will take you. Themo will come with me – back to the OP. We'll meet you in two days' time. Can you carry your own AK?'

On the tar road Steve will be able to move on his own if guided along; they can make quick time and be five kilometres away before first light. Most importantly, he and Da Silva will leave no tracks.

The mood among the four men changes. Suddenly there is hope; they can get their wounded buddy out of there. Jo-Jo pulls out his map and spreads it on the ground. Crouching down with Da Silva, he uses his passive beta light to locate an outstanding feature as their RV point roughly five kilometres to the west. Since the terrain becomes mountainous to the west, there is no shortage of prominent landmarks. Jo-Jo points out a protruding feature in the escarpment and they quickly agree on scheduled radio calls and RV procedures.

Jo-Jo and Themo stash their remaining water and emergency rations in the radio bag along with the medical pack. Da Silva passes his flare bag to Themo and heaves the radio pack on. Wasting no further time, he helps Steve to his feet and starts guiding him towards the road that is barely 50 metres away.

While Themo clears away any sign that might have been left, Jo-Jo listens out for vehicle movement on the road but all seems quiet. Then they move out in the direction of the OP, Themo carrying Da Silva's bag and Steve's combat webbing which they have decided to discard later.

They have moved about one kilometre when the radio crackles to life. The lead pilot's voice comes across sounding calm and in control, 'Alpha, this is Bravo, do you copy?'

'Bravo, this is Alpha, read you loud and clear,' *Jo-Jo responds.*

'Any updates for me?' *the pilot asks. To Jo-Jo the man sounds so relaxed he could be sitting with a cup of tea chatting to his wife.*

'Yes, sure. It's a beehive.' *Referring to the first flare that would have been planted on run-in he says,* 'Foxtrot One is not active. I say again, Foxtrot One not active!'

'Copy that,' *the pilot says,* 'Go ahead.'

'The others are active but you can expect some action.'

They both know what the implications are. The air base is exceptionally well protected. Early warning and tracking radars are deployed on the high ground to the south, while defence missile systems and anti-aircraft will be brought to readiness as soon as the alarm is sounded.

'Okay, that's our business, we'll deal with that. What about you?' *Jo-Jo knows that the pilot needs assurance that the team is safe but would not make any reference over the radio that could compromise them.*

'It's BLACK FOREST from our side,' *he says, using the pre-arranged code word to clear the attack. It means the* team has moved out of the area and that the attack can commence.

'Copy that. Call you in ten ...' the pilot responds.

Jo-Jo realises that the bombers will commence with the attack in the next ten or 15 minutes. He moves up to Themo and quietly instructs him to take the lead and get them as high up the mountainside as possible in the available time. They soon start climbing and Jo-Jo keeps listening out on the VHF.

Morning has started to break above the eastern horizon and first light is less than 20 minutes away. It is critical for them to reach the OP before the enemy can react. They also need time to ensure their equipment is properly camouflaged and to find a suitable hide-away.

When the radio crackles to life again, the pilot's voice comes in hushed tones, 'Okay, ROUND HAT in five ... four ... three ... two ... one.'

Neither Jo-Jo nor Themo have expected the spectacular show that suddenly erupts in the direction of the target. Two massive flames leap up in unison from the darkness below, literally reaching hundreds of feet into the sky, even momentarily illuminating the two operators on the mountainside.

The next moment the sound of the approaching fighters reaches them – at first it's a steadily growing drone but within seconds it turns into a deafening crescendo. In a massive real-life display of fireworks the anti-aircraft guns from the target open up, sending innumerable streaks of light across the night sky.

The first wave of bombers clears away as quickly as

they have arrived but Jo-Jo knows the attack has only just begun. The next wave comes even more unexpectedly as the target is now abuzz with activity and explosions. The team only realises that a second and third wave have commenced once the bombs start exploding.

It is over as suddenly as it has started. The lead pilot's voice comes across faintly, 'Bravo, this is Alpha, do you copy?'

But Jo-Jo does not bother to answer as he realises that, since all the aircraft have departed, a strong signal might indicate the team's presence in the area and could compromise their position. He manages to catch the gist of the pilot's brief report: 'Packages delivered, most on target. We have one limping goose. Going home.'

They reach the location of the OP as first light dawns. They circle around to approach from the higher ground above and take time to observe the site before moving in. Their equipment is intact and undisturbed. From the OP they can see scattered fires and rising smoke in the direction of the air base but it is still too dark to identify any details on the runway.

They use the time to remove the second HF radio, the remaining water and most of the remaining rations from Da Silva's and Steve's packs and re-pack them in their own ruck-sacks. Then they carry the two half-empty packs and Steve's combat webbing down the slope and stash the equipment in dense undergrowth at the bottom of the mountain, covering it all completely with sand and dry leaves.

Back at the OP they find a hole under a protruding rock face that is big enough for both of them to hide in, their packs hidden in cavities among the rocks close by. Themo does a final sweep of the area to ensure that no sign is left. After checking that Jo-Jo is camouflaged and their position secured, he crawls in besides his team leader. They settle in for a long day of waiting and watching.

Although they can only partially see the air strip, it soon becomes clear that extensive damage has been caused. They see aircraft burning at the eastern end of the runway, while huge columns of black smoke that rise from the western side indicate that the bombs have also found their target there. Throughout the day no fixed wing aircraft take off or land but by 11:00 two MI-24 Hind D attack helicopters suddenly appear overhead, circling the escarpment at low level, often hovering barely 50 feet above their position. Twice they see troops in a sweepline passing below them, moving slowly and shouting commands as they traverse along.

However, more troubling to the team is the sound of voices from above. For most of the day commands are being shouted from somewhere on the escarpment above their position. At times the voices come very close. Since they are not able to see beyond the rock up the slope, their only option is to remain absolutely still and vigilant. Both of them have their weapons in the firing mode and a hand grenade ready for quick action.

While Jo-Jo is tempted to get the HF out and report their position, he realises that it would be too dangerous. He can only hope that Da Silva and Steve have reached a safe position and that José has reported the situation by now. At around 13:00 Jo-Jo indicates to Themo that he has to take photos. The bush around them has become quiet; for some time they have not heard any voices.

Jo-Jo retrieves the camera from his runaway bag and eases himself out of their hiding place to get a better view. He realises that details on the photos will be limited due to the restriction caused by the vegetation but it is important that he captures some of the destruction on the runway. He manages to get a few general images of the columns of smoke rising up from the target, then zooms in on a burning aircraft and takes a series of shots.

Finally the day wears out. They dare not move until after dark, as the enemy would most likely have deployed listening posts along the edge of the mountain. At 22:00 they finally crawl out, stiff, sore and hungry but elated that they have not been discovered and have been able to witness the damage caused by the attack.

They move out silently, leaving the packs of Da Silva and Steve behind in their hiding places as they are too bulky to carry. Once down the mountainside, they take care to circle around the enemy positions at the bluegums towards the tar road. They reach the road just before 23:00 and decide to move next to the road in case the enemy has established road blocks.

Their vigilance is soon rewarded; they have moved barely two kilometres west along the road when they pick up light and movement through the lens of their night vision goggles. For fear of stumbling onto early-warning positions in the dark, they swerve off the road and take a 90-degree bearing north into the bush. It takes them an hour to circle around the road block. Once they reach the tar road on the western side, they can clearly make out a cluster of vehicles and temporary shelters in the direction from which they have come.

Jo-Jo decides to take the risk of walking on the road to gain some distance before first light. They cover another three kilometres and then move straight into the uneven terrain on the southern side of the road – the very hills Da Silva would have headed for. They find a suitable hide and bed down for the remainder of the night.

When Jo-Jo switches his VHF radio on the next morning, Da Silva answers immediately, his voice loud and clear, indicating that they must be in close range of each other. A description of the terrain features makes them realise they are barely 300 metres apart. Da Silva has left Steve in a hide at the bottom of a hill and has climbed to the top to observe the area and to establish VHF comms with his team leader.

They decide to stay in their positions until nightfall, however, a precaution that turns out to save their lives, as by 08:00 the area is alive with troops. An armoured vehicle patrol consisting of four BMP-1 infantry combat vehicles slowly passes on the tar road while foot patrols sweep the bushline on both sides of the road.

From his position high up on the hill, Da Silva is able to observe the enemy activities and relay the information to Jo-Jo. Twice a foot patrol passes dangerously close to Jo-Jo and Themo's position but they are well hidden and have left no sign of their presence. As soon as it turns dark, Da Silva moves down from his position and the two teams close in on each other.

It turns out Steve's condition is stable. While his burn wounds are no better, he has limited eyesight in one eye and can distinguish light and shapes. During the day Jo-Jo has worked out a route that will take them to a pick-up point 20 kilometres due south of their position. However, it means that they will have to negotiate the rough and uneven terrain with their wounded buddy.

Themo suggests that they improvise a stretcher but they discard the idea as it implies that two of them will be tied down while carrying their buddy. Silent movement and anti-tracking will be virtually impossible. Another major concern is their water and food situation. From experience Jo-Jo knows that carrying their comrade through the thickly vegetated and uneven terrain would soon take its toll; they would be out of water in a matter of hours.

The only alternative is to move another ten kilometres west on the tar road until they reach a dry riverbed stretching far into the rocky terrain to the south of the road. Jo-Jo encourages Steve while he treats his wounds, talking him through the plan and explaining their emergency procedure if they run into trouble.

Themo will move in front on the road with Jo-Jo close behind. They will be carrying the packs while Da Silva and Steve bring up the rear, 100 metres behind. If anything goes wrong, Da Silva will immediately pick Steve up in a fireman's lift and move into cover on the left side of the road, leaving the two in front to engage the enemy or apply evasive action. The crash RV will be 100 metres due south from the point where Da Silva and Steve leave the road.

Once on the road Themo takes the lead without any word from Jo-Jo. Da Silva has led Steve to the tarmac and now places Steve's hand onto his own shoulder. He keeps his radio's handset ready and guides his buddy to catch up on the pace. It takes them a while to get the hang of things but once they have found a rhythm, the going becomes easier. Jo-Jo has allowed Themo to move ahead at the front as he knows that nothing will escape the scout's superb senses.

They keep a slow but steady pace to ensure that their injured buddy keeps up. The march passes without incident and by 03:00 the next morning they approach the valley along which the dry riverbed runs at right angles with the road. Jo-Jo cautions the team not to leave any tracks as they move into the sparse undergrowth.

This is a critical juncture and they all know that the smallest mistake could be fatal; if their tracks were to be found leading south along the riverbed, the enemy would immediately know their intentions. With a wounded team member and water down to less than a litre per person, the margin for escape would be extremely narrow.

While they take a much-needed rest Jo-Jo shares his plan with the others. Steve is to don Themo's anti-track booties so that Da Silva, also wearing anti-track covers, can guide him down the dry riverbed. Jo-Jo and Themo will scout ahead, sticking to the rocky surface on both sides of the narrow valley. By first light they will be in an OP overlooking the riverbed to determine if the enemy has located their tracks and launched a follow-up.

On Jo-Jo's cue, Themo uses a freshly picked branch

to carefully wipe out any signs they might have left as they move away from the road. After 200 metres he takes up the lead opposite Jo-Jo on the river bank. The going is relatively easy and they cover about three kilometres before daybreak, then move away from the river into the mountains.

Once the team has settled into a hide in a shallow valley, Jo-Jo and Themo move up the mountainside to keep a watch on their route. Jo-Jo also takes the HF set along to bring the tactical headquarters up to speed. If their tracks are followed, he would need to activate a telstar (an aircraft designated to fly at high altitude outside the danger zone to establish communications with the team) and set the Air Force's E&E plan in motion. If not, he will arrange a pick-up by helicopter for the following night.

They have barely settled into their OP when Themo reports movement down in the riverbed. An enemy patrol consisting of around ten soldiers is slowly moving along the route they covered earlier that morning, clearly on edge and scanning the mountain slopes for signs of an ambush as they move along. It dawns on Jo-Jo that it is too early in the day to pick up a scrap as the enemy would have the whole day to launch a follow-up; there was no way they would be able to carry Steve out and survive on their remaining water.

He quickly sets up the HF set and transmits an emergency call. Jo-Jo detects the desperation in Det's voice as he responds on the very first signal, 'This is zero, I read you loud and clear. Anything to report?'

The last the tactical headquarters has heard from the

team was the previous day when Da Silva dispatched a brief message. They have obviously been worried about the situation on the ground and have been eagerly awaiting a call. Jo-Jo has hastily prepared a DET message indicating their position and confirming they are all together. He now adds a cryptic note that they might be followed and may need extraction later that day, then transmits the message.

They watch the enemy patrol as they approach the point at which the team left the riverbed that morning. The soldiers stop. Only some of them are visible but it is clear that they are not moving along the valley any longer. Jo-Jo calls Da Silva on the VHF radio and tells him to get ready; the enemy patrol might be moving in on their tracks. Then he briefs Themo on their actions; once the enemy has been locked in contact with Da Silva, they will move in from the high ground for a side attack, engaging the combatants at a 90-degree angle and picking them off from the side.

They have just packed up the HF radio and are about to start moving, when a long drawn-out whistle from the direction of the enemy patrol draws their attention. Jo-Jo catches Themo's expression from the corner of his eye and sees a broad grin spreading across his buddy's face.

'What's up? Let's go. There's no time …' he whispers.

But Themo is not moving anywhere. He points down the mountain to where the soldiers have gathered up their kit and are moving out in formation, clearly intent on continuing their patrol down the riverbed. It appears that they were merely taking a rest at the very point where the team exited from the valley that morning.

Jo-Jo waits until they have disappeared around the mountainside before he instructs Da Silva to stand down. Very relieved he prepares an extensive message to bring HQ up to speed with all the developments of the last two days while Themo gets the radio out and rigs the antenna.

At around 15:00 that afternoon they observe the same patrol moving back along the riverbed, this time in single file and obviously worn out. This is Jo-Jo's cue; tonight they will move out and cover the best part of the way to an LZ that has been identified 20 kilometres further south during their E&E planning. They will take care not to step on the tracks of the enemy patrol, thus ensuring that their own tracks will not be noted the next morning.

He realises that their window of opportunity is narrowing rapidly; they are nearly out of water and Steve urgently needs medical attention. With their wounded buddy, the only route out is along the dry riverbed. They will only have one chance.

Once the two of them have joined Da Silva and Steve at the hide, they start making preparations for the night's march. While Jo-Jo treats Steve's wounds, Da Silva collects all the remaining water in one bottle. He will keep the water with him to try and maintain Steve's hydration levels throughout the night. Their survival now depends on whether they can get their injured comrade to the LZ before they completely run out of water – or before the enemy patrols return the next day.

They start out as soon as it is dark. For the first few kilometres they manage a steady pace but Steve is getting weaker with every step as the dehydration and shock of his wounds take their toll. By midnight they have to give it up as their buddy starts hallucinating. He has struggled to maintain even the slow pace Da Silva has settled down to. Twice he lost his grip on Da Silva's shoulder and fell, causing him much pain and making him shout out in agony.

They carry him, taking turns. Da Silva hauls him onto his back and slogs on for a kilometre while the other two forge ahead with the packs. Then they switch, each taking a turn to carry Steve to safety. By now their buddy is in extreme pain as his burn wounds are rubbing against the back of the person carrying him but they have no option but to push on through the night.

By daybreak they reach the area of the LZ. Exhaustion and thirst have driven them to the brink but each one knows that they dare not relax their vigil; no tracks can be left as they move out of the valley and ascend the mountain ridge overlooking the LZ.

They find a good spot in a dense thicket for the day's hide. Da Silva pitches the antenna while Jo-Jo sends Themo up to the highest point to keep watch. Then he sets about caring for Steve, gently tending his wounds and reassuring him that they will soon be home. Steve is weak from dehydration and fever. Jo-Jo uses the last bit of water sparingly to wet his lips and tongue.

While they were on the move it was impossible to insert a drip line but now that he knows that they will be static for the day, Jo-Jo decides to insert a saline drip to keep their comrade hydrated. He struggles to find a suitable vein but finally succeeds. Then he injects two ampoules of Sosegon *pain killers and watches as his buddy slowly relaxes and falls into a deep sleep after about 30 minutes.*

During their scheduled radio call with the tactical head-quarters (tac HQ), Jo-Jo dispatches a detailed summary of events. He ensures HQ that Steve is okay and the pick-up is confirmed for 19:00 that evening. The only message from the tac HQ is that they have to guarantee the safety of the LZ before the helicopters are dispatched at 17:00.

The day drags on. No enemy is reported but a few times they hear the sound of MI-24 gunships north of them. Thirst has now become their main enemy as exhaustion threatens to immobilise them. Their tired bodies desire only to rest but Jo-Jo and Da Silva force themselves to remain vigilant by sitting up and facing each other. Themo remains in his OP.

In the afternoon they use a canvas ground sheet and two poles to improvise a stretcher to carry Steve to the helicopter. By 16:00 Da Silva carefully conducts a patrol around the perimeter of the LZ, checking for any sign of enemy presence. All seems quiet and by 16:45 Jo-Jo transmits an 'all clear' message to the HQ.

Finally, just before last light, they hear the sound of the Pumas approaching from the south. Themo has come down from his OP and positioned himself on the opposite side of the LZ. Steve, now awake and fully conscious, has been placed on the stretcher. He has insisted on walking but Jo-Jo has refused. 'We must pretend you are in a bad way so they give us the TLC treatment,' he has joked.

He talks the lead pilot in to their position. No smoke grenade is required as the pilots recognise the position on run-in. The first helicopter touches down and they swiftly carry Steve to the door where willing hands reach out to take him on board. Once their buddy is safely on board and away, the rest of them wait for the second chopper to land.

Jo-Jo watches while the other two clamber on board before he climbs in. Then they are up and away and the ground rushes past as the night enfolds them.

Once back at Fort Rev, a Special Forces base within the confines of Air Force Base Ondangwa, Steve is rushed to the sickbay. The rest of the team gather for a 'hot debrief', a wrap-up of the sequence of events while it is still fresh in their minds.

The hot debrief is attended by the regular tac HQ staff and Kokkie automatically takes charge of proceedings. A special aircraft has brought Colonel Yalo, Major Thabo and an engineer from MECSUP all the way from Pretoria. Also in attendance are an Air Force colonel as well as the lead pilot of the attack force, both from the regional headquarters at Oshakati. While the atmosphere is somewhat subdued due to Steve's predicament, the undercurrent seems to be one of optimism.

Kokkie spends a few minutes to welcome everyone and summarise the objectives of the mission before he intro-duces the team leader. Using the operational map with the team's progress brightly marked on an overlay, Jo-Jo takes the audience through the operation from infiltration to extraction. A debate ensues when he relates the events around the premature detonation of the flare but Colonel Yalo cuts everyone short, insisting that the debrief is not the place for speculation or accusations and that a proper investigation would be launched into the malfunctioning of the device.

When Jo-Jo gets to the point where comms was established with the lead pilot of the attacking aircraft, Kokkie asks the pilot to describe the attack. The story unfolds like a scene from a war movie as the pilot explains how they initially engaged a 'passive' target – until seconds after the initial strike the sky erupted in a wall of tracers. They delivered no less than 48 high-precision bombs.

Radio intercepts indicated that 11 aircraft, mostly fighters, were totally destroyed while more than 25 others would need repairs before they would be able to take to the skies again. The runway is in a complete state of disrepair.

Jo-Jo then describes how he and Themo observed the target amidst an angry and aggressive enemy and finally, how the team painstakingly sneaked their wounded comrade out of the danger zone to the pick-up point.

The rest of the debrief is spent on a SWOT analysis of the whole operation as the team summarises strengths and weakness before and during the deployment, as well as opportunities and threats predicted for future missions of similar nature. Once Kokkie has concluded the proceedings, Colonel Yalo wraps up by congratulating the pilots and thanking the team for a job well done.

◆

🔆 KEY LEARNING: USE EQ TO STRENGTHEN THE TEAM!

Emotional intelligence, also known as emotional quotient (EQ), forms the basis for critical skills that are required to perform well in the workplace. Among these are assertiveness, empathy, social skills, communication, stress tolerance, decision-making and teamwork. In an article published in *Forbes* magazine, Travis Bradberry, co-author of *Emotional Intelligence 2.0*, said, 'Emotional intelligence is the single biggest predictor of performance in the workplace and the strongest driver of leadership and personal excellence.'

Jo-Jo showed empathy when he responded to Steve's apology by saying, 'It's not your fault, Steve. It's the equipment. Come on, we'll get you out of here.'

Imagine if Jo-Jo, or one of the other team members, had said something like, 'Yes, Steve, you are right, it was your fault and you almost compromised the whole mission!'

This would have impacted negatively on all the team members and would have had a direct influence on the team's performance at the most critical time.

Similarly, Jo-Jo combined assertiveness with a healthy sense of humour when, in Chapter 5, he conveyed his final decision on who should penetrate the base to Themo: 'Because I say so. And because I navigate better than you. And because I don't have a wife and kids who will make your life miserable when I'm dead.'

According to Lowri Dowthwaite, a lecturer in

psychological interventions at the University of Central Lancashire, humour can be used to enhance relationships, reduce conflict and get people to listen when you communicate a message or an instruction. Our young captain understood that a light-hearted and humorous response would take the sting out of a decision that could otherwise be perceived as tough.

A leader who is emotionally connected to her team will note when team members are taking work or personal strain. She will then respond appropriately to the situation, either directly with the individual or within the group. This will make a difference in the performance of the team as it will indicate that the leader really cares. The same goes for individual team members.

When a big service delivery company restructured, three new senior managers were appointed in the service delivery department. The individuals in these roles would be the conduits between the business executives and the teams that had to deliver the required services.

This not only required excellent planning and organising skills but also that they be assertive, as well as excellent communicators. Furthermore, they needed to have empathy and well-developed social skills – they had to be able to handle stressful situations, listen to various inputs before making a final decision, rally teams behind a common cause and get them to walk the extra mile.

Each senior manager was allocated a portfolio to look after. Planning and resource allocation started and soon afterwards, execution. Two of the areas tracked well on delivery but one area was in trouble. The team kept losing team members and just could not gain traction – delivery almost came to a complete standstill. This caused the business executives to lose confidence, not only in the ability of the senior manager responsible for the poorly performing portfolio but also in the entire service delivery department.

Something had to be done. Closer inspection revealed that the senior manager lacked the basic yet critical EQ skills. He would call people useless to their faces and accuse them of lying in front of their colleagues. He wasn't prepared to take any responsibility when things went wrong but was eager to take credit when the team did well.

Team members simply could not work in the environment created by this senior manager and either transferred to another department or left the company. Owing to his lack of EQ the senior manager and his teams did not perform, costing the company dearly.

 KEY LEARNING: ADAPT WHEN THINGS CHANGE!

Adaptability is one of the nine characteristics required by a Special Forces operator. During your career it is inevitable that you will encounter setbacks or that you will have to deviate from the original plan due to a change in circumstances. It is important on a personal and team level to deal decisively with the situation at hand to ensure that objectives are still achieved.

The premature detonation of the flare did not only change the situation for the Special Forces team on the ground but it also changed the situation for the Air Force attack team that was already in the air and close to the target. The way that the relevant teams reacted to the setback still ensured a successful outcome, even though they had to adapt their plans.

Once, Victor was part of a four-man team who worked for a leading company in the gaming and hospitality industry. The team leader, Adrian, was a well-respected leader and gave excellent guidance to the team. He was instrumental in the planning stage and was key in developing the approach that eventually allowed the team to complete the work in a much shorter time frame than usual.

Being the team leader also meant that he controlled the interaction with the client and dealt with the commercial arrangements. The team executed the first phase of the project – a small and short deliverable – successfully.

Unbeknownst to the team, Adrian had designed this phase in such a way that the team had to rehearse the approach. This resulted in a forming, storming and norming process that saw them reach a high-performing state in a short space of time. Team morale was high and the team made good progress on phase two until one morning they woke up to the news that Adrian was shot and killed by an intruder at his home.

The team was devastated as some of them also considered Adrian to be a dear friend. Still, the discipline instilled by Adrian made them realise they had to adapt to this new reality and complete the job. The team selected a new leader among them, after which they re-planned the project and re-allocated responsibilities. They finished the job on time.

💡 KEY LEARNING: DEBRIEF AND OPTIMISE!

The quickest way to create distrust and anxiety in teams is to launch a witch-hunt to identify a culprit and apportion blame when something goes wrong. Allow team members to make mistakes.

People will be hesitant to make decisions or to perform optimally if they expect to be persecuted. Rather conduct an honest review of what went wrong and allow individuals to learn from it. Consider mistakes from the bright side: the wrongs are invariably countered by a number of things that went right! In the case of our Special Forces team, while the flare detonated prematurely and Steve got injured, the bombing raid was still successful.

The other side to this coin is an over-inflated ego as a result of success. Take care to stay humble when successful. Boasting about successes, becoming complacent and having an over-inflated ego can be as damaging as an unsuccessful project.

It is important to give clear orders and create a sense of purpose and direction before a mission. In order to optimise, however, it is equally important to debrief and determine strengths and weaknesses on completion of the mission. In Chapter 3 Jo-Jo provided a briefing of the mission to everyone in a clear and concise message.

During the 'hot debrief' all the role players got together and unpacked the mission. Our team's preparation and rehearsals had gone well, the deployment went according to plan and no one was injured during the parachute jump. While executing their mission the team exercised extreme discipline, stayed focused on the task and said no to possible distractions that might have caused them to lose focus. The skills they were taught during training were applied effectively.

Water did run critically low towards the end of the mission, which could have become a problem had the team not been extracted. The first aid kit contained the required medical supplies that were used to treat Steve's wounds.

One thing did go wrong during the deployment, however – the flare malfunctioned, wounding their buddy and almost jeopardising the mission. Could the premature detonation have been prevented by introducing a second check of all the steps before the pin was pulled? Was the equipment faulty? Captain Yalo decided to address the matter at a later stage to prevent it from happening again in the future. They then moved on to the impact of the bombing and concluded that the required objectives were achieved.

As much as the operational briefing determines the success of a mission, the debriefing captures lessons learned and determines the success of future deployments. For the debrief, all role players should be called together to review each stage and activity of the project to identify successes and failures.

Thoroughly reviewing a completed project and asking the critical questions will enable a team to update standard operating procedures or techniques that will enhance the success of similar future projects, or possibly save lives.

The only producer of silicon carbide in Africa had issues with the quality and quantity of their end products. They asked Victor and a team to assist. Silicon carbide, also called synthetic moissanite or simply moissanite, is a rare mineral with similar properties to diamonds. It is transparent and hard, 9–9.5 on the Mohs scale, compared to 10 for diamond.

Industrial clients use silicon carbide in the manufacturing of sanding paper and for ceramic parts where very high endurance is required, such as car brakes, car clutches and ceramic plates in bulletproof vests. Since silicon carbide is also a semiconductor it has electronic applications and is used in light-emitting diodes (LEDs) and in electronic devices that operate at high temperatures or voltages.

Victor and a team member conducted an initial assesment at the company to gather information and establish an understanding of the manufacturing process and the challenges involved. The acquired information, together with a suggested solution approach were documented and presented to company management for approval. The solution approach was approved and a small team of five was put together and briefed on the approach and the objectives of the project. Three of the team members had worked together before and two were new to the company and the existing team members.

The detailed brief, which lasted half a day, provided a common cause that everyone could rally around. The team completed the detailed planning together and allocated responsibilities and tasks. It must also be mentioned that all the individuals were highly experienced specialists. The team went through the team development phases in a short time frame and soon started to deliver good results.

One of the focus areas for improvement was the furnace (oven) build activity. A furnace base is constructed with a specific mixture of small crushed material, including two upright electrodes at either end of the furnace consisting of graphite that are connected to an electrical energy source. It is critical to ensure the width, height and radius of the furnace base is constructed as per specification.

The furnace base must be levelled before the graphite core is inserted to connect the two electrodes (think of this as the filament in an electrical bulb). The levelling of the furnace base takes several hours. A specific mixture of raw materials is inserted on top of the graphite core. The furnace is then fired up and left to cook, reaching temperatures of between 1 600 °C (2 910 °F) and 2 500 °C (4 530 °F) in the core. The materials sublimate (transition to a new form) to form the required end products.

During the detailed analysis and observations the team concluded that there seemed to be variation in the way the furnaces were built and further variation between the teams that built them. The biggest portion of variable costs could also be attributed to the furnace-building activity.

The engineers decided to meet with some of the employees on top of one of the furnace bases in a typical 'Chinese parliament' fashion to gather input and suggestions. One high tech option was the use of military grade tablets linked to a geographical positioning system to display the furnace build steps electronically, allowing the supervisor to capture progress along the way. Warnings should then generate if the outputs are not within the specifications. Another solution was to develop a mechanical machine to build the furnace base based on a template, eliminating human error.

Then one of the employees, a quiet person, spoke up: 'Why don't we use some of the quartz (it is white in colour) and mark the furnace base to form a template? Once the base is built, we can dump some material on the side and drive one of the big front-end loaders on top of the furnace, lower the bucket and level the base.'

A brilliant suggestion from the least expected corner! A few other suggestions were also adopted and the standard operating procedures (SOPs) were updated before a dry-run (rehearsal) was scheduled.

The results exceeded expectations. Quality and quantity increased. Cost reduced and the time to build a furnace also decreased significantly.

A debrief after the project revealed that one of the reasons for the success of the project was the way in which the brief was presented and conducted at the start of the project. This method was adopted as the new standard on future projects, which increased the probability of success significantly.

A few final key points:

- ☐ Use emotional intelligence and humour in an effective and meaningful way to develop relationships and deal with challenging situations.
- ☐ Sometimes things don't go according to plan – diagnose, adapt, communicate and advance to achieve your objectives.
- ☐ Schedule a debrief with all the relevant parties after each successful and unsuccessful project, to continually improve. Stay humble and keep that ego in check.

7

LEADERSHIP

A personal perspective on leadership in the Special Forces – by Koos Stadler

The drama that unfolds around Captain Jo-Jo and his team in this book is the real-life story of a South African Special Forces team during a typical deployment. The challenges Jo-Jo faced, the hardships he endured and the often difficult decisions he had to make, are all real. It is the story of a Special Forces team leader. It is also my story.

Leading by example has been a way of life for me. I have done numerous reconnaissance missions as team leader, having had to locate and observe targets in enemy-held areas. Initially I served as a team leader with the recce wing of 31 Battalion, a Bushman unit stationed in the then Caprivi Strip during the Border War, from where we were deployed on tactical reconnaissance missions into neighbouring countries that harboured insurgent groups.

Then I did the Special Forces selection and training cycle and ended up as team leader with what was then known as 5 Reconnaissance Regiment, later renamed 5 Special Forces Regiment. For five years I had the honour of serving with 54 Commando, the sub-unit dubbed 'Small Teams' on account of the size of the teams that conducted extremely sensitive and highly specialised missions deep into hostile territories.

During these recce missions, I had to penetrate no less than six well-protected strategic enemy installations. Even where I had the choice to let others do the infiltration, I opted to do the stalking myself – in spite of my own fears and uncertainties. I made a conscious decision not to show my fear.

I was successful in most missions. Where jobs were not successfully completed, I was granted the grace to return home unharmed, albeit a bit shaken on some occasions.

At 5 Special Forces Regiment I was nominated best team leader for three consecutive years. While initially our bands were small and the task of leading them relatively simple, the size of the groups steadily expanded and I gradually acquired the skills to lead larger and more composite military teams.

During my 24-year Special Forces career I commanded a number of sub-units and finally founded and took command of a full-scale training unit, the Special Forces School north of Pretoria. It became the first unit in the South African Army to register a formally recognised qualification with the country's National Qualifications Framework and as such became a model for training units across the country. I also had the privilege of serving as senior staff officer responsible for training (SSO Training) and later as SSO Operations at Special Forces Headquarters.

As class leader on a number of military courses I was exposed to the challenges of leading my peers. On my Senior Command and Staff Course I was elected

'Beagle', or student leader, during a very demanding time right after the abolishment of apartheid and in the midst of major transformation in our Defence Force.

As the student leader I had two significant challenges. Firstly I had to manage a group of senior people, each with their own perception of right and wrong and focus them on a common course.

The second and more pronounced challenge was to bring diverse groups together in an environment representing the new South Africa. On the course were newly integrated officers from mixed backgrounds (some from uMkonto we Sizwe, the ANC's military wing, some from the Pan Africanist Congress and some from the erstwhile homelands such as Transkei and Ciskei) – mostly colonels and a few generals – while the rest of the students were lieutenant-colonels. The group now represented the true demographics of South Africa, not just the white population.

In the extremely polarised society of the time, the role of Beagle turned out to be a highly demanding one. There were hard-core racists at both ends of the spectrum who invariably forced me to revert to my fall-back mode – the old Special Forces attitude of 'Fit in or f off'. In the end it all worked out as the course was concluded successfully!

I learned a very important leadership lesson right at the start of my Special Forces career. The first posting I somewhat reluctantly had to accept upon completion of the Special Forces selection and training cycle, was with the then

51 Commando at Fort Rev in Ondangwa, on the border between then South West Africa and Angola. 51 Commando's exclusive task was to do 'pseudo' operations, where the teams had to act like SWAPO insurgents and attempt to infiltrate their ranks. Most of the soldiers had actually been SWAPO cadres before.

After they were captured, they went through a process of interrogation and indoctrination and were then given the option of either being held captive or 'turned' to fight against their own. Since there was a fair amount of money and some benefits such as free medical care involved – as well as the insurance that their families would be taken care of – the majority opted to turn.

But for me the environment was new and somewhat peculiar. Not only did I have to face the challenge of cross-cultural leadership, I also had to deploy with people I did not trust. Moreover, the ex-cadres had a completely different approach to tactics since they applied the doctrine followed by the insurgents. Weapons were slung across the back while they walked in very relaxed patrol formations and visited every settlement they passed.

Their tactics were in direct confrontation with my strict Special Forces training. It was a time of constant conflict. While I attempted to drill some elementary tactical concepts into the group, their reaction was – understandably – that these 'Boere tactics' would reveal their identity and blow their cover among the local population.

I was regularly deployed alone on missions with groups of ex-SWAPO cadres. I recall one deployment where we had to take along a SWAPO terrorist who had been 'turned' barely two weeks earlier to lead us to the location of an upcoming meeting between two insurgent groups. Without his knowledge, the firing pin of his AK-47 had been disengaged. I was extremely vigilant and literally slept with my one eye open at night, always away from the group, always in a well-chosen spot with a carpet of dried leaves underfoot – to warn me if someone was approaching.

My biggest challenge was that the old and trusted 'lead by example' concept could not be applied – at least not from my perspective. Owing to my distinctly European features (in spite of being covered in brown camouflage cream and sporting an 'Afro' wig) I was always kept out of sight and could never venture close to the population or the insurgents we were supposed to meet. I also discovered that my team would feed me information very selectively.

The missing ingredient in this relationship was trust. I did not trust the ex-terrorists; they did not trust the young, inexperienced white lieutenant suddenly thrust upon them. In addition, I never learned the skills to cope with a situation where there is a lack of trust, with the result that I found it impossible to instil discipline or lead the way I saw fit, through my own example. And the backdrop to all of this was my one clear mission – the reason I had joined Special Forces in the first place: I wanted to join Small Teams. I did not want my objective compromised by anything.

I share this 'failure' because there was a lesson to be learned. There were operators who were exceptionally successful in leading the pseudo teams. I envy them, because I never reached a point where I could accept the differences I considered fundamental and adapt accordingly. I only realised, years later, that if I had had the sense to apply situational leadership in all its manifestations, as discussed below, I might have succeeded in leading the pseudo teams.

After literally begging the authorities for months on end to let me join the Small Teams sub-unit, I was finally released after a year with 51 Commando and was ready to fulfil my lifelong dream. I found my niche with Small Teams, among like-minded men with the same sense of purpose. I accepted full and unconditional ownership for my decision – a trait that was ingrained by my parents since childhood. Accepting complete ownership would become the foundation of my operating career from then on.

In their bestseller, *Extreme Ownership: How U.S. Navy Seals Lead and Win*, authors Jocko Willink and Leif Babin describe how leaders who take absolute ownership, 'not just of those things for which they were responsible but for everything that impacted their mission' were the most exceptional and how 'These leaders cast no blame. They made no excuses. Instead of complaining about challenges or setbacks, they developed solutions and solved problems.'

To take full ownership for both your successes and failures, was indeed at the core of every small team operator's belief system.

Leadership is not something you do to people; it's something you do with them, says Ken Blanchard in his book *The Leadership Pill*. Leadership in Small Teams came easily to me, partially perhaps because of the size of the group but mainly because everyone was a leader in his own right and had the same vision.

During deployments Chinese parliament sessions were frequently used to make decisions (this term was never used at the time; it was only coined later after various training exercises with the British SAS). The concept proved exceptionally effective to garner specialised input and to convert it to action. It is as simple as getting the team together, discussing the problem, gathering everyone's input, making a collective decision on the most sensible solution and then acting on it. Sometimes the person with the lowest rank or least experience has the best solution as he may approach the problem from a different perspective. I have often experienced how the best solution came from the least expected corner.

As Captain Jo-Jo had to say no to some instructions in the interest of his team, on occasion I had to say no to the authorities. It takes courage to question authority or to challenge the status quo but it is more important to do the right thing. Do not hesitate to stand up and say NO if that is your conviction.

I believe that I was always dealt a fair deal and had only myself to blame if things went wrong. I have my own code of conduct that I attempt to live by, to this day. With the grace of God, I have always relied on the following set of principles:

☐ As a leader, I have always believed in honesty and integrity.

☐ Self-discipline has been a non-negotiable.

☐ I have cared for my team members more than I've worried about myself.

☐ I believe in the good of man, that every human being has a unique skill set that would benefit the greater body. As such, I have always inspired my men to do the best they can.

☐ I have always been humble, both about my position as leader and my achievements.

☐ A healthy dose of humour has always served me well. While humour is seldom a permanent solution, it has certainly helped me to diffuse stressful situations or take the sting out of harsh words. The ability to see the funny side of any situation will invariably help to soften the impact and buy time to find more permanent solutions.

The leadership philosophy in Special Forces

For as long as warriors have been led into battle by some of their own, leadership in the military has been a much-debated subject. The nature of leadership has continued to evolve throughout history as soldiers have faced the challenge of an ever-changing battlespace.

The demands of modern-day combat place increasingly heavy burdens on the shoulders of military leaders, whether it be in conventional war or the so-called non-linear or asymmetric conflicts, where extraordinary countermeasures have to be applied to combat insurgents

that use irregular and unconventional met
9/11 terrorist attack on the World Tr
example). The same demands are imposed upon
Forces soldiers in the field, implying that leaders have to
be selected and trained to live up to these demands.

Special Forces worldwide continue to achieve extraordinary results with teams from different backgrounds,
races, religions and beliefs. Outstanding leadership is the
ability to achieve goals sustainably through inspired people who have the ability to overcome obstacles within a
diverse and constantly changing environment. Successful
teams require leaders with the right qualities who apply
relevant techniques and make appropriate decisions.

In an organisation the main responsibility of a team
leader is to ensure that the team produces the required
deliverables in terms of quality, cost and safety within
a set time frame. This establishes a causal link between
team leader effectiveness, team effectiveness and overall
organisational performance. In Chapter 1 we discussed
how outstanding team leaders will help teams achieve
the required objectives in the most effective way and
that poor leadership contributes to the degradation of
team effectiveness. In this chapter we explore leadership
in the Special Forces and how organisations can benefit
from it.

Special Forces operations demand effective leadership
at every level. Resourcefulness, innovation and enthusiasm
by junior leaders, who act beyond the immediate control
of senior commanders, are expected and encouraged. In
the Special Forces team, achieving success in operations

depends largely on the capacity of junior leaders to motivate, inspire and then command subordinates in dangerous and sometimes chaotic circumstances.

The Special Forces doctrinal publication *Philosophy of Leadership* states that, 'Effective leaders in Special Forces are fair, approachable, of high integrity and compassionate. They have vision and a passion to fulfil that. Effective leaders require physical and moral courage, professional competence, confidence and the resilience to respond to setbacks in order to continue to pursue organisational goals until they are successful.'

Special Forces units place great emphasis on the assessment and selection of their young leader corps. It is therefore important that equal emphasis be placed on the development of leadership skills among them.

A further element of leadership development in Special Forces is the concept of role models at the junior levels. Take the example of Major Kokkie de Koning in our story. Kokkie didn't challenge Jo-Jo on any of his choices but guided him in setting up a framework for his time-versus-task schedule. In a similar vein Sergeant-Major Det guided Da Silva with the preparation of the tactical radios but left the responsibility for drafting the operation's communication plan with him. The high quality of junior officers, team leaders and trainers within the operator corps – and their influence on others – is a characteristic of these units.

In the Special Forces leadership has always been based on the following three concepts:

☐ Mission command
☐ Transformational leadership
☐ Situational leadership

The three concepts are an integral part of Special Forces philosophy because they encompass all the essential elements of leadership required in the field. The approach to leadership, the principles required to ensure success, as well as the required characteristics of the individual, are best explained through an analysis of the three concepts.

MISSION COMMAND

Mission command is a style of military command that combines centralised intent with decentralised execution – it promotes freedom, speed of action and initiative. Subordinates who understand the commander's intentions, their own missions and the context of those missions are told what effect they are to achieve and the reason why it needs to be achieved. They are then given the means and allowed the freedom to execute the commander's intent.

Mission command firstly requires a specific attitude of mind or an approach where the commander takes the initiative and aims for originality and surprise. The very nature of specialised operations, coupled with the uncertainty and chaos of combat, implies that Special Forces operations demand improvisation, initiative, freedom and speed of action. Decentralised command, the delegation of responsibility and the provisioning of resources to the appropriate level are essential to the success of operations.

The following three elements are the building blocks of mission command. Without them, the term is meaningless:

- ☐ Timely decision-making
- ☐ Understanding the superior commander's intention
- ☐ A clear responsibility to fulfil that intention

In practice, mission command follows these basic steps:

- ☐ A commander ensures that his subordinates understand his intentions, their own missions and the strategic, operational and tactical context.
- ☐ Subordinates are told what effect they are to achieve (desired end-state) and the reason why it is necessary.
- ☐ Subordinates are allocated sufficient resources to carry out their missions.
- ☐ A commander exerts minimum control so as not to unnecessarily limit his subordinates' freedom of action.
- ☐ Subordinates decide for themselves how best to achieve their missions.

Jo-Jo's commanding officer made the purpose and mission objectives clear when he provided his warning order. The purpose of the mission was to disrupt the staging of aerial attacks on own troops and save lives. Jo-Jo also provided a clear and concise directive when the time came to brief his team.

The very essence of leadership is the ability to mobilise people around a mutual goal and to get them to direct their energy into fulfilling that goal. It is important that teams know what their destination is. It is the job of the leader to make sure that the goal is clearly articulated in an inspirational manner. The leader needs to communicate with meaning.

In Special Forces, if an officer's orders are misunderstood, it is considered his fault. Never make the mistake of assuming that all information conveyed was assimilated. Keep the language simple, use metaphors that capture the imagination and repeat often, because repetition ingrains the concept in the mind.

It is said of Napoleon that before every battle he would call in a corporal (the lowest-ranking non-commissioned officer), read his orders to him and ask him to interpret what those orders meant. If the corporal's response was accurate, Napoleon knew that every other officer and non-commissioned officer in his army would most probably know what to do.

In line with the 'decentralised responsibility' advocated by mission command, Jo-Jo had the freedom to select his own team members. The manner in which the mission was to be achieved was also up to him. The relevant resources were then made available to meet the requirements of the team. The initial operational instruction from headquarters recommended a six-man team but Jo-Jo's preference for a pure reconnaissance mission was a two-man team. Eventually, however, he selected a four-man team based on the mission objectives that included the planting of flares.

General Colin Powell, chairman of the US Joint Chiefs of Staff during the First Gulf War and later US Secretary of State, famously said, 'If soldiers stop escalating problems to you, they might have lost confidence in your ability to lead them, or worse, concluded that you simply do not care.'

This is a failure of leadership. He added, 'When a captain came in to see me, I would tell the youngster to sit down and say, "Talk to me, son, what have you got?" And then I'd let him argue with me. I would do everything I could to let him think he was arguing with an equal, because he knew more about the subject than I did.'

Good leaders make themselves accessible and available. And they listen. Colonel Tim Yalo chose not to argue with Jo-Jo when he informed him that the team would consist of four operators instead of the recommended six. Yalo accepted the suggestion unconditionally and also conveyed this message with confidence to his superior officer. Trust was the key ingredient.

Empowering people in an environment where there is high trust can assist an organisation to overcome enormous obstacles and deliver the required objectives. Trust enables a team to follow a plan more easily or react to a crisis decisively.

The command staff were always in close proximity to provide the required guidance and coaching. This was the case when the warning order was given to Jo-Jo and the team, when the detailed plans were put together and when the preparation and rehearsals were conducted. While the young captain had the confidence to make his own decisions and certainly did not have to be spoon fed, it must have been reassuring to know that his superiors had his back.

TRANSFORMATIONAL LEADERSHIP

Studies of over 1500 general managers, military officers and church ministers have shown that transformational leaders run highly effective organisations, work units and projects, which perform at the highest level of competitiveness.[1] Transformational leaders have better relationships with their superiors, peers and direct reports. They have become known for making a greater contribution to the organisation than those who rely solely on transactional leadership.

Conversely, colleagues exert a greater amount of extra effort when working with transformational leaders. They exhibit a higher level of persistence at solving problems,

---

1 The Full-range Leadership model serves as the basis for leadership in Special Forces (as defined by BM Bass and BJ Avolio). The concept of transformational leadership as described in the Full Range model is advocated as the ideal foundation for leadership development.

are more willing to take intellectual risks and produce a higher range of creative products.

Organisations led exclusively by transactional leaders are generally less effective and less innovative, particularly if leadership is applied passively and reactively in a management-by-exception style (intervening only when standards are not met). Transformational leaders run organisations that focus on continuous improvement and strive towards total quality management. They create high-performance teams that accomplish extremely challenging objectives.

Transformational leadership is achieved by the four Is, namely individualised consideration, intellectual stimulation, inspirational motivation and idealised influence. These components require a closer look.

Individualised consideration: An essential challenge for Special Forces leaders at all levels is to allow time and energy to work with each team member. The leader must be able to diagnose the needs of each member, while at the same time realising that each member has different needs, desires and capabilities. The leader must not only focus on the team members' current needs but also attempt to develop them to higher need levels in order to maximise their potential.

Individualised consideration therefore entails recognising individual needs as well as elevating them when the time is right. This type of leader assumes that each individual in his team has different needs and desires, identifies the individual's strength, shows empathy for the person's situation, targets an area to develop and to elevate individual needs. He also follows up and tracks performance and development, establishes a plan to address potential work overload and links the needs and abilities of the individual to current and potential job challenges.

Jo-Jo picked his team based on the team members' individual strengths. These attributes were applied during the mission to ensure success and although the situation was extremely stressful at times, he showed empathy and took time to motivate each of them. Jo-Jo was also cognisant of the team's energy levels and the distances to be covered; therefore he called rest intervals at appropriate times. Good leaders know that team members can't run at breakneck speed all the time. Similarly, the leader cannot expect his team to constantly produce high-level results without a requisite rest period.

While a balanced approach is important, it does not simply boil down to having 'work-life balance'. In fact, the term is an anomaly, as it implies that work is work and life is what happens outside the workplace. Work can and, in fact, should also be fun. In essence there are six areas or dimensions that demand attention: Financial (your business or career), family (your loved ones), social (friends and the world out there), mental (your personal development), physical (your health) and spiritual (your relationship with your Creator).

Success in one area can never compensate for failure in another. Life is a much more complex journey where all six dimensions deserve equal attention. While success in one is of course praiseworthy, neglect or failure in another may result in unhappiness. If, for example, a person's profession becomes the be-all and end-all of his or her existence, the end result may be hollow and empty.

Leaders should encourage team members to nurture all six dimensions and guard against a style of leadership where members start taking an approach that success at work is the only and ultimate goal.

Any organisation that allows its most valuable resource, people, to burn out is doomed. Employees will either reach a point where they collapse or rebel against the system. Depending on the demands of the mission, there will be the occasional 14-hour day stretch or the odd working weekend. But that should never become the norm. Leaders should recognise that people have interests beyond the work space and should encourage them to maintain a balance in their lives.

As a leader, try to have some fun and maintain a healthy balance in your team! In the long haul, the balanced leader will always beat the one-dimensional workaholic.

Intellectual stimulation: In the ever-changing and dynamic world of Special Forces operations, it is essential that leaders encourage their teams to question the status quo and improve on techniques continually and vigorously. This type of leadership requires a different state of mind. When we forget to question conventional wisdom and the institutions such wisdom supports, stagnation may be imminent and the seeds for failure may already be planted.

Intellectually stimulating leaders encourage their

teams to take intellectual risks, to be creative and to question the assumptions underlying the way they operate. Such leaders provide their teams with a new lens to view the world around them and to solve problems in an innovative manner.

Behavioural indicators of this type of leader are that she discards traditional ways of thinking and acting. She doesn't use threats or create friction to help question the 'old' way of doing things but sparks team members' thinking by getting them to 'imagine what if', encourages members to rethink their ideas in the light of new information and provides a unique angle or perspective to analyse current or potential problems. She encourages the team to empower themselves with knowledge, does not hesitate to engage in conversation and even argues with members of the team.

Mature leaders don't view their subordinates as potential threats to their authority. Instead, they constantly encourage independent thought, innovative action and forthright, open expression. Another of Powell's famous sayings is: 'This particular emperor expects to be told when he is naked.'

Leaders should, in fact, tolerate rebels who have the audacity to challenge the status quo. Encourage your team to give their honest views and also to tell you when they think you are about to screw up. Encourage them to raise issues and problems. The only rule should be that they approach you with a 'solution mentality': 'You are welcome to bring me any problem, as long as you propose at least one solution.'

Themo challenged Jo-Jo and Da Silva on whether they were the best choice for the penetration of the enemy air base. The fact that Themo had no reservations to question his leader's decision shows that Jo-Jo had created the environment for open communication and did not feel threatened by Themo's challenge. Intellectual stimulation means that the leader recognises each team member's independent train of thought.

Inspirational motivation: The third 'I' provides the required energy to overcome obstacles which at first may seem insurmountable. Such leadership elevates the expectations and desires of team members commensurate with the mission.

Inspirational motivators, through their words and actions, instil confidence in the course and inspire team members to perform to the best of their abilities. These leaders are able to call teams and individuals into action by introducing appropriate challenges that simply must be met.

Some behavioural indicators of this type of leader are that she offers the team a sense of mission and purpose, raises the expectations of the team, calls for action by the team, introduces new challenges, focuses team members on what is essential for success, takes necessary risks, helps to envision exciting new possibilities, inspires through her words and actions and does not hesitate to lead by example.

Jo-Jo led by example and was the first to jump when the aircraft reached the drop zone. He inspired the group. People will follow the leader if they are convinced he is worth following; that is, if they believe his ideas are sound and that he knows the route. This is especially true if they are set on achieving the same goals.

Depending on the particular circumstances, the goal could be something very simple or something very big and inspirational, so powerful that it moves people's souls. A good leader gives his team perspective and elevates the job to a bigger purpose, for example by saying, 'Are we laying bricks or are we building a mosque or cathedral to the honour of God?'

So many great leaders of the past had the ability to inspire. Nelson Mandela mobilised an entire nation to face their differences, to forgive the sins of the past and to become a unified nation. Don't hesitate to unleash the inspirational motivator within you to mobilise your team!

Idealised influence: The fourth 'I' of transformational leadership represents, at least to a degree, a culmination of the other three. It is also somewhat more complicated than the other three in the sense that it is based both on the reaction of team members to their leader, as well as on the leader's behaviour.

Idealised influence is generally characterised by high levels of trust in the leader and faith in what he is attempting to accomplish. In essence idealised influence comes down to the charisma a leader has, whether team members enjoy being with the leader and like to be associated with his values and norms.

This type of leader is seen as being more capable of

handling unusual situations. He exhibits a great deal of confidence and assurance that the plan to solve a crisis is feasible – if everyone in the team works together. Such leaders seek out ways to build team members' confidence that their objectives can be met. They are virtually always described by their team members as extremely persistent, particularly when faced with overwhelming odds.

Leaders who are often described as 'charismatic' tend to have an extraordinary ability to influence their teams. This type of leader will attempt to improve and develop individual members. Some behavioural indicators of this type of leader are that she shows a great deal of confidence and persistence that the objectives will be met by the group as a whole, engenders trust in the individuals' ability to overcome crises, demonstrates the importance of knowing where the team should be going, displays an inner-direction that keeps members on course, develops dedicated and loyal team members through consistence of action and individual support to each member and considers her own personal achievement as being based on the achievement of others.

Such a leader also has the ability to anticipate the future, becomes a role model for team members, sets high standards towards which teams will aspire willingly, moves members to go beyond their own self-interest for the good of the team, is outspoken, forthright and persevering in an effort to attain ideals and inspires through words and actions.

SITUATIONAL LEADERSHIP

While not specifically a leadership style, situational leadership is promoted within Special Forces for the simple reason that it is highly applicable. The situational theory of leadership refers to when the leader or manager of an organisation has to adjust his style to fit the development level of the team members he is trying to influence. It also suggests that no single leadership style is best.

In Special Forces the concept has been slightly adapted to imply that the person best suited for the job at hand should adopt the leadership role. Since every person within the team is a leader in his own right, it is expected of every member to take command of a situation in which he stands out as the natural leader.

There have been numerous examples of this in Special Forces but an applicable one from our story is when Steve took command of the team who had to plant the second flare. However, when Steve got injured, Themo immediately adopted the role of leader. This approach links closely with the ability to accept full responsibility – extreme ownership – as described earlier, an attribute that forms part of each Small Team operator's mental skill set.

Situational leaders learn to demonstrate four core, common and critical leadership competencies:

☐ Diagnose – understand the situation he is trying to influence.

- ☐ Adapt – adjust his behaviour in response to the contingences of the situation.
- ☐ Communicate – interact with others in a manner they can understand and accept.
- ☐ Advance – manage the dynamics resulting from the situation.

More specifically, situational leaders:
- ☐ Maintain an acute awareness of their innate leadership-related strengths and areas for development within the team.
- ☐ Understand when a particular leadership style has a high probability of success by testing it with subordinates.
- ☐ Skilfully influence up, down and across the organisation by knowing when to be 'consistent' and when to be 'flexible'.
- ☐ Create more productive teams by accelerating the development of individuals that are new to their role and are learning a new task.
- ☐ Develop engaged, committed team members by effectively recognising and proactively addressing the dynamics of performance regression.
- ☐ Effectively drive behaviour change and business results by communicating through a common, practical language of leadership.

Different situations require different styles of leadership. At times, for example in a life-or-death combat situation, leadership needs to be authoritarian and commands are shouted at subordinates (there is no time to question orders or to contemplate action). In other situations a consultative approach may produce the best results, to tap the team's collective input and to ensure understanding and buy-in. A good example was when Jo-Jo made use of the Chinese parliament to get his team's input when they had to get Steve to safety after he had been injured during the premature detonation of the flare.

The leader should have the sense to adapt his style and apply situational leadership to suit the demands of the situation. But in the final analysis it is all about getting the job done – the ultimate priority of the leader. Even if circumstances are ideal and a people-oriented approach is followed, the leader still fails if the goal is not achieved.

As a leader you cannot always please everyone. Leaders who are not able to make tough and unpopular decisions; or adjust to the situation, lack one of the essential elements of decisive leadership. Leadership involves taking responsibility for the ultimate goal and the welfare of the group, which means that some people might at times get angry about the leader's decisions.

However, if leaders have to choose between the ultimate goal and not hurting individuals' feelings, the latter has to take second place. Leadership is not a popularity contest. Trying not to offend anyone will set leaders on the road to mediocrity and eventual failure. Ultimately, a good leader knows that gaining respect is more important than being liked and performance is more important than popularity.

Conversely, earning the team's respect and driving them to top performance usually breeds loyalty and even affection. When the leader asks followers to take risks to achieve a certain goal – in a combat situation to risk death – respect and the team's inherent capability to perform become indispensable resources.

We have described how mission command, transformational leadership and situational leadership can be used to achieve extraordinary results. These leadership styles together with the character of a Special Forces team leader provide the essentials to lead small teams in the military as well as in organisations.

◆

A personal perspective on leadership in business – by Anton Burger

As co-author Koos Stadler wrote earlier in this chapter, success in Special Forces operations depended largely on the capacity of team leaders to motivate, inspire and then command teams in dangerous and chaotic circumstances. In the business world teams should also be led by leaders who can inspire and motivate team members to strive, achieve and thrive!

When I approached Koos to write this book with me, leadership was one of the fundamental principles at the back of my mind. While I firmly believed it was a guiding principle of successful teams, I was unsure how we would discuss it in the book. The answer revealed itself gradually as the story of Captain Jo-Jo and his team unfolded – it became clear that the visionary leadership portrayed by our Special Forces team leader is what also makes the difference in the corporate world.

For most of my working life as a management consultant I had a new job every six to 12 months. It was both a blessing and a curse. On the one hand it exposed me to a variety of situations, people and challenges. On the other the time spent on the job came at the expense of family time.

Over the years on the numerous consulting projects I was involved with I have seen true leadership in action. I believe that strong leadership is the core element of every successful team. My premise is that if you have an effective team leader, you have an effective team. During projects I often had to adopt the role of team leader and guide the team to make the right decisions and execute the task in accordance with their plan. I have shared some of these experiences through the character of Victor.

It took me the better part of my career to learn how to lead teams and get the required results – and finally a book to collect my thoughts. And still I am learning.

I had the privilege to become closely involved in the daily mechanics of project teams, often having to guide team leaders to exert their leadership skills and achieve their full potential. Where I was involved with failed projects, I took full ownership no matter what the cause. When things went well and the team achieved success, I felt proud to be part of it but always attributed it to the team effort.

I have first-hand experience of managing a small team in a company that achieved the impossible. Based on that success, I was appointed as the leader of a much larger team to achieve the same. I failed spectacularly! This was also the point in my life where I started asking the key questions that we have tried to answer in this book.

I believe that, in order to lead others, you must know yourself and be able to control your thoughts and actions. To get to this point, you require exposure to successes and failures. I was lucky that the majority of leaders in my life were great people, from whom I learned a great deal and who made me who I am today. To those leaders I am forever indebted. There were a few who were not so great but to them I am equally indebted as they taught me what *not* to do.

Over the years I have had to teach myself, with some help, to identify when I move into Red Head status and calm myself down to Blue Head status. This assisted greatly and many punch-ups turned into constructive problem-solving sessions. Every now and then my amygdala still gets the better of me but then I walk over to my colleague and apologise.

I also realised that people can flourish under one type of leader and fail dismally under another. Aspirant leaders invariably learn from their role models. Unfortunately this could mean that negative traits or bad habits are copied.

In the business world a 'mission command' style of management creates the same atmosphere and positive attitudes as in a military environment. All of the successful projects I was involved in were based on centralised intent with decentralised execution, with the relevant autonomy to make decisions. I also experienced the power of the Chinese parliament to come to decisions.

The fundamentals of transformational leadership are also applicable in business. I have always developed good relationships with team members and chosen to be emotionally connected to them. I was willing to teach and share some of my own experiences where I could but I also realised how important it is to be open to learning from your team members.

I have always cared for my team members to the extent that I sometimes sacrificed bonuses and salary increases rather to reward and recognise team members. My motto was to motivate and lead from the front and get people to believe in themselves.

In private enterprise situational leadership is also a major requirement. Adjusting my leadership style to fit the development of people helped me to get the most out of them. This approach often saved the day.

I was fortunate to experience unconditional trust from my business partners for the best part of my consulting career and from fellow executive members in my first corporate job after I left the consulting world. I saw the power trust brings when, in times of need, you have to focus on the problem at hand and not worry about someone undermining you or betraying your trust.

This book is also testament to the trust created in the small writing team that consisted of just me and Koos. We created a virtual team, who had to achieve a certain goal within a specific time frame while being thousands of kilometres apart. We started writing the book without having known each other before or even meeting face to face (that only came a few months later). The engineer in me took over and we put a plan and design together. I guess the countless times we had to rewrite chapters can be described as our rehearsals. We pretty much stuck to the plan but the important part was that each person delivered what he said he would and when he said he would.

Strength of character and the associated attributes of integrity and courage are not only crucial in situations where Special Forces soldiers have to make decisions that could change the course of history but also in any kind of team context within organisations. True character is based on a strong value system that informs an individual's behaviour – it is the result of established beliefs and values.

Commanders at all levels in Special Forces are expected to have strength of character which means they should display honesty, integrity, self-discipline, confidence, perseverance, dependability, conscientiousness, excellent people skills and a strong work ethic. These are attributes worth copying from role models in private enterprise. They indeed form the cornerstone of leadership in business.

In conclusion, great leaders are rarely alone. However, a sense of loneliness is endemic to leadership at any level and in every enterprise. All matters considered, once the leader has listened to his team it is up to him and nobody else, to make the decision and accept full responsibility for the consequences.

In a combat situation, the ability to make the final decision fearlessly becomes paramount. 'The buck stops here' President Harry Truman used to say – a man who had to make perhaps the toughest and most extreme military decision of all time – whether or not to drop the atom bomb on Hiroshima.

Everyone in an organisation is called on to make sacrifices – of time, of energy, of effort. But the leader has to make a sacrifice of a special kind – he or she must live with the suspense as well as the aftermath of the decision: did I make the right call? The leader must sacrifice himself to serve as role model, knowing that he will be under immense scrutiny.

True leadership means balancing authority, power, influence, delegation and responsibility to enable individuals and groups to pursue and reach their goals and those of the organisation.

EPILOGUE

Teams are at the centre of organisations. In many ways the success of these organisations depends greatly, often completely, on teams that perform well. Organisational performance and growth are therefore directly linked to the performance of teams.

Whether you are putting together a new team, or trying to enhance the performance of an existing one, the key learnings in this book will assist you in this process. As a first principle, it is important to get the right people with the right skills for your team. Selecting the right team is a prerequisite for success. Invest in a process that allows for the scientific selection of team members and you will soon reap the benefits.

You also need to invest in practical training because adults learn best when theory is put into practice and they experience for themselves how a different approach yields a better solution. Include continuous training and self-improvement techniques to ensure that your team members consistently perform at their optimum. Practice makes perfect.

When compiling your team, apply the golden rule: go small! While there is comfort in numbers, you may find the converse – discomfort in small numbers – to be beneficial to your team's performance. Team members are inclined to perform better when they feel responsible and do not have the luxury of people around them to rely on. There is no proven number or ideal size for the team but it needs to be as small as the situation allows – and big enough to ensure the task is executed effectively.

Create a code of conduct for your team. Discuss the rules on a regular basis within the team and personally address team members who have not adhered to them. Be sure also to recognise those who behave in the desired way. Create an *esprit de corps* and let it flourish. The organisation will be rewarded in the most unexpected ways. Allow comradeship to become the vehicle that carries the team to success and remember, trust is a must! Without trust teams will fail to perform at their best.

Teams need to plan and rehearse together to unleash the potential of each team member. Plan for each key contingency and adapt when the situation changes. It is important to provide clarity of purpose and direction as everyone needs to know where they are going and why they are involved in the initiative. A clear understanding of the purpose will enhance the level of engagement of team members and will ensure that everyone knows what they need to take responsibility for. The team leader should visualise the end state and inspire team members to own it.

Make sure the prerequisites for successful execution are in place, then create magic! Stay focused on your original objectives, get buy-in from everyone if the objectives change and have the discipline to say no to additional tasks. Measure performance in regular short intervals and manage it. Take time to assess risks and plan for every possible scenario to increase the probability of success and avoid surprises.

Use the leadership qualities and emotional intelligence embedded in your team to build relationships, both inside the team and with external partners. Find ways to influence external parties and get them to cooperate to achieve your goals. Then reciprocate!

On completion of a project, whether it was successful or not, it is always wise to debrief the team and all the key role players involved properly in order to optimise future projects. Along with the debrief and the regular short management intervals, it is important to recognise individuals who have performed well and even reward them where possible. After all, team members are the DNA of an organisation and recognition of their efforts will increase their sense of ownership.

Charismatic, visionary and assertive leadership is the one element that has made the difference in all successful Special Forces operations. When Ken Blanchard wrote, 'Leadership is not something you do to people, it's something you do with them,' he might not have had the Special Forces small team in mind but he certainly understood the necessity for leaders to be at the centre of the action – to take the team along after accepting responsibility as leader. Transformational leaders will always be at the core of every successful venture.

Just as every person is unique, every team differs and has its own distinctive dynamics. While we might not have the answer to all challenges a team may encounter, we believe the key learnings presented in this book will assist team and business leaders to lead their teams to success and guide individuals to become high-performing team members.

The key learnings and leadership principles shared in this book are not new and have been discussed in different books, journals and papers. What is the team secret then? It lies in applying them all together. It is to understand the role each one plays in the context of a high-performing team.

These principles have assisted us greatly in the Special Forces environment and the corporate world. We hope they will work for you, too!

ADDENDUM: Great 8 Competencies

The competency sets below were taken from the SHL Universal Competency Framework™ Profiler and Designer cards (copyright© 2004 by SHL Group plc, reproduced with permission of the copyright holder). These titles may be freely used for research purposes subject to due acknowledgement of the copyright holder.

Below is a description of the Great Eight Competencies and their 20 competency dimensions:

GREAT 8 COMPETENCY	COMPETENCY DIMENSION	COMPETENCY DESCRIPTION
Leading and Deciding	Deciding and Initiating Action	Takes responsibility for actions, projects and people; takes initiative and works under own direction; initiates and generates activity and introduces changes into work processes; makes quick, clear decisions which may include tough choices or considered risks.
	Leading and Supervising	Provides others with a clear direction; motivates and empowers others; recruits staff of high calibre; provides staff with development opportunities and coaching; sets appropriate standards of behaviour.
Supporting and Cooperating	Working with People	Shows respect for the views and contributions of other team members; shows empathy; listens, supports and cares for others; consults others and shares information and expertise with them; builds team spirit and reconciles conflict; adapts to the team and fits in well.
	Adhering to Principles and Values	Upholds ethics and values; demonstrates integrity; promotes and defends equal opportunities; builds diverse teams; encourages organisational and individual responsibility towards the community and the environment.

GREAT 8 COMPETENCY	COMPETENCY DIMENSION	COMPETENCY DESCRIPTION
Interacting and Presenting	Relating and Networking	Easily establishes good relationships with customers and staff; relates well to people at all levels; builds wide and effective networks of contacts; uses humour appropriately to bring warmth to relationships with others.
	Persuading and Influencing	Gains clear agreement and commitment from others by persuading, convincing and negotiating; makes effective use of political processes to influence and persuade others; promotes ideas on behalf of one self or others; makes a strong personal impact on others; takes care to manage one's impression on others.
	Presenting and Communicating Information	Speaks fluently; expresses opinions, information and key points of an argument clearly; makes presentations and undertakes public speaking with skill and confidence; responds quickly to the needs of an audience and to their reactions and feedback; projects credibility.
Analysing and Interpreting	Writing and Reporting	Writes convincingly; writes clearly, succinctly and correctly; avoids the unnecessary use of jargon or complicated language; writes in a well-structured and logical way; structures information to meet the needs and understanding of the intended audience.
	Applying Expertise and Technology	Applies specialist and detailed technical expertise; uses technology to achieve work objectives; develops job knowledge and expertise (theoretical and practical) through continual professional development; demonstrates an understanding of different organisational departments and functions.
	Applying Expertise and Analysing	Analyses numerical data and all other sources of information, to break them into component parts, patterns and relationships; probes for further information or greater understanding of a problem; makes rational judgements from the available information and analysis; demonstrates an understanding of how one issue may be a part of a much larger system.
Creating and Conceptualising	Learning and Researching	Rapidly learns new tasks and commits information to memory quickly; demonstrates an immediate understanding of newly presented information; gathers comprehensive information to support decision-making; encourages an organisational learning approach (i.e. learns from successes and failures and seeks staff and customer feedback).

Great 8 Competency	Competency Dimension	Competency Description
Creating and Conceptual- ising (continued)	Creating and Innovating	Produces new ideas, approaches, or insights; creates innovative products or designs; produces a range of solutions to problems. Works strate- gically to realise organisational goals; sets and develops strategies; identifies, develops positive and compelling visions of the organisation's future potential; takes account of a wide range of issues across, and related to, the organisation.
Organising and Executing	Planning and Organising	Sets clearly defined objectives; plans activities and projects well in advance and takes account of possible changing circumstances; identifies and organises resources needed to accomplish tasks; manages time effectively; monitors performance against deadlines and milestones.
	Delivering Results and Meeting Customer Expectations	Focuses on customer needs and satisfaction; sets high standards for quality and quantity; monitors and maintains quality and productivity; works in a systematic, methodical and orderly way; consis- tently achieves project goals.
Adapting and Coping	Adapting and Responding to Change	Adapts to changing circumstances; tolerates ambiguity; accepts new ideas and change initia- tives; adapts interpersonal style to suit different people or situations; shows an interest in new experiences.
	Coping with Pressure and Setbacks	Maintains a positive outlook at work; works productively in a pressurised environment; keeps emotions under control during difficult situations; handles criticism well and learns from it; balances the demands of a work life and a personal life.
Enterprising and Performing	Achieving Personal Work Goals and Objectives	Accepts and tackles demanding goals with enthusiasm; works hard and puts in longer hours when it is necessary; seeks progression to roles of increased responsibility and influence; identifies own development needs and makes use of devel- opmental or training opportunities.

BIBLIOGRAPHY

Books:

Bartram, D 2008, 'Work profiling & job analysis' in N Chmiel (ed.), *An introduction to work and organisational psychology: a European perspective*, 2nd edn, Blackwell Publishing, Malden, Mass.

Bass, BM & Avolio, BJ 1994, *Improving organizational effectiveness through transformational leadership*, Sage Publications, Thousand Oaks, CA.

Bossidy, L & Charan, R 2002, *Execution: The discipline of getting things done*, Currency, New York.

Burke, R 1999, *Project Management: Planning & control techniques*, 3rd edn, Promatec International, Cape Town.

Cloud, H 2006, *Integrity: The courage to meet the demands of reality*, Harper, New York.

Collins, JC 2001, *Good to Great*, William Collins, New York.

Covey, SR 1999, *The Seven Habits of Highly Effective People*, Simon & Schuster, London.

Glasl, F & Ballreich, R 2004, *Team and organisational development as a means for conflict prevention and resolution*, 2nd edn, viewed 22 May 2018, <http://www.berghof-handbook.net>

Gryna, FM, Chua, CH & Defeo, JA 2007, *Juran's*

Quality Planning and analysis, 5th edn, McGraw-Hill, New York.

Hersey, P & Blanchard, KH 1977, Management of organizational behaviour, 3rd edn, *Utilizing Human Resources*. Prentice Hall, New Jersey.

Kerr, J 2013, *Legacy: What the All Blacks can teach us about the business of life*, Constable, London.

Kolb, DA 1984, *Experiential learning: Experience as the source of learning and development*, Prentice Hall, Englewood Cliffs NJ.

Le Blanc, P, De Jonge, J & Schaufeli, W 2008, 'Job Stress and Occupational Health', in N Chmiel (ed.), *An introduction to work and organisational psychology: a European perspective*, 2nd edn, Blackwell Publishing, Malden, Mass.

Maxwell, JC 2002, *Teamwork makes the dreamwork*, Thomas Nelson, Nashville, Tennessee.

McChesney, C, Covey, S & Huling, J 2012, *The 4 disciplines of execution: Achieving your wildly important goals*, Free Press, New York.

McRaven, WH 1996, *Spec Ops: Case studies in special operations warfare - theory and practice*, Random House Publishing Group, New York.

Sinek, SO 2014, *Leaders eat last: Why some teams pull together and others don't*, Nota, Kbh.

Smit, PJ & Cronjé, GJ de J 2002, *Management principles: A contemporary edition for Africa*. 3rd edition, Juta, Cape Town.

Sonnetag, S, Niessen, C & Ohly, S 2008, 'Learning and training at work', in N Chmiel (ed.), *An introduction to work and organisational psychology: a European perspective*, 2nd edn, Blackwell Publishing, Malden, Mass.

Stadler, K 2015, *Recce: Small team missions behind enemy lines*, Tafelberg, Cape Town.

West, MA 2008, 'Effective Teams in Organisations', in N Chmiel, (ed.), *An introduction to work and organisational psychology: a European perspective*, 2nd edition, Blackwell Publishing, Malden, Mass.

Willink, J & Babin, L 2015, *Extreme ownership: How U.S. Navy Seals lead and win,* St. Martin's Press, New York.

Articles / Essays / Papers / Reports:

Adams, BD, Webb, RDG 2001, 'Trust in Small Military Teams', HumanSystems Incorporated, Guelph, Ontario.

Barchas, P 1986, 'A sociophysiological orientation to small groups,' in E Lawler (ed.) *Advances in group processes*, vol. 3, pp. 209–246.

Bartram, D 2005, 'The Great Eight Competencies: A criterion-centric approach to validation', *Journal of Applied Psychology 2005*, vol. 90, no. 6, pp. 1185–1203.

Bartram, D 2012, 'The SHL Universal Competency Framework', *SHL White Paper*, pp. 1–10.

Bradberry, T 2014, *Emotional intelligence is the other kind of smart,* viewed 22 May 2018, <https://www.forbes.

com/sites/travisbradberry/2014/01/09/emotional-intel-ligence/#572f3541ac0e>

De Jager, K & Harris, I 2017, 'The conscious way, leader as coach,' viewed 22 May 2018, <www.theconsciousway.co.za>

Dowthwaite, L 2017, 'Funny people are more intelligent than their po-faced peers', *The Conversation*, viewed 22 May 2018, <https://theconversation.com/funny-people-are-more-intelligent-than-their-po-faced-peers-84709>

Gurdjian, P, Halbeisen, T & Lane, K 2014, 'Why leadership development programs fail', *McKinsey Quarterly*, January 2014, pp. 1–6.

Hoegel, M 2005, 'Smaller teams – better teamwork: How to keep project teams small', *Business Horizons*, vol. 48, pp. 209–214.

Hoegel, M, Parboteeah, KP & Gemuenden, HG 2003, 'When teamwork really matters: Task innovativeness as a moderator of the teamwork-performance relationship in software development projects', *Journal of Engineering and Technology Management*, vol. 20, pp. 281–302.

Johnson, LK 2008, 'Exerting influence without authority', *Harvard Business Review*, viewed 22 May 2018, <https://hbr.org/2008/02/exerting-influence-without-aut>

Kravitz, DA, & Martin, B 1986, 'Ringelmann rediscovered: The original article', *Journal of Personality and Social Psychology*, vol. 50, no. 5, pp. 936–941.

McCarthy, M 2010, 'Experiential learning theory: from

theory to practice', *Journal of Business & Economics Research*, vol. 8, no. 5, pp. 131–140, viewed 22 May 2018, <http://www.cluteinstitute.com/ojs/index.php/JBER/article/viewFile/725/710>

Schrage, M 2015, 'Reward your best teams, not just star players', *Harvard Business Review*, viewed 22 May 2018, <https://hbr.org/2015/06/reward-your-best-teams-not-just-star-players>

Films:

Up the Yangtze 2008, motion picture, directed by Yung Chang, produced by Mila Aung-Thwin, John Christou, distributed by Zeitgeist Films (USA) and Dogwoof Pictures (UK), and starring Jerry Bo Yu Chen, Cindy Yu Shui, and Campbell Ping He, viewed 22 May 2018, <https://www.youtube.com/watch?v=D0ToMQZPl4s>

Personal Communication Pieces:

Smit, I 2011, pers. comm., 'On leadership, Lessons from the military', May.

Interviews:

Kaiser, C 2017, Interview with Anton Burger

Bedeker, F 2017, Interview with Anton Burger

Venter, A 2018, Interview with Anton Burger

INDEX